Patterns
For Living
From the Old Testament

By A.L. and Joyce Gill

ISBN 0-941975-39-8

*Powerhouse Publishing
P.O. Box 99
Fawnskin, CA 92333
(909) 866-3119*

Books By A.L. and Joyce Gill

God's Promises for Your Every Need
Destined for Dominion
Out! In the Name of Jesus
Victory over Deception

Manuals In This Series

Authority of the Believer
*How to Quit Losing
and Start Winning*

The Church Triumphant
Through the Book of Acts

God's Provision for Healing
*Receiving and Ministering
God's Healing Power*

The Ministry Gifts
*Apostle, Prophet,
Evangelist, Pastor, Teacher*

Miracle Evangelism
God's Plan to Reach the World

New Creation Image
Knowing Who You Are in Christ

Praise and Worship
Becoming Worshipers of God

Supernatural Living
Through the Gifts of the Holy Spirit

About the Authors

A.L. and Joyce Gill are internationally known speakers, authors and Bible teachers. A.L.'s apostolic ministry travels have taken him to over fifty nations of the world, preaching in person to crowds exceeding one hundred thousand and to many millions by radio and television

Their top-selling books and manuals have sold over two million copies in the United States. Their writings, which have been translated into many languages, are being used in Bible schools and seminars around the world.

The powerful life-changing truths of God's Word explode in the lives of others through their dynamic preaching, teaching, writing and video and audio tape ministry.

The awesome glory of the presence of God is experienced in their praise and worship seminars as believers discover how to become true and intimate worshipers of God. Many have discovered a new and exciting dimension of victory and boldness through their teachings on the authority of the believer.

The Gills have trained many believers to step into their own God-given supernatural ministries with the healing power of God flowing through their hands. Many have learned to be supernaturally natural as they are released to operate in all nine gifts of the Holy Spirit in their daily lives and ministries.

Both A.L. and Joyce have Master of Theological Studies degrees. A.L. has also earned a Doctor of Philosophy in Theology degree from Vision Christian University. Their ministry is solidly based on the Word of God, is centered on Jesus, strong in faith and taught in the power of the Holy Spirit.

Their ministry is a demonstration of the Father's heart of love. Their preaching and teaching are accompanied by powerful anointing, signs, wonders, and healing miracles with many being slain in waves under the power of God.

Signs of revival including waves of holy laughter, weeping before the Lord and awesome manifestations of God's glory and power are being experienced by many who attend their meetings.

**A.L. and Joyce Gill are dedicated to producing practical tools for equipping believers to do the works of Jesus.
Their desire is to promote victorious, supernatural living for every believer at all levels of Christian maturity.**

A Word to Teachers and Students

When we accept Christ, we are launched into an exciting new life – for many of us a totally new way of living. We begin studying our Bibles and learning from many teachers. New Christians are often encouraged to skip to the New Testament for study, and for the new Christian, this is good advice. However, the Bible can never really be understood in bits and pieces. Each part is inter-related to the others.

We could picture the Bible as a huge jigsaw puzzle. The teachings we receive are wonderful, but they are like groups of pieces put together, but not fit into the total picture. We receive nuggets of revelation, but again, they are just part of the whole picture.

Many Christians cannot truly understand the New Testament because they have not received teaching on the foundations which are laid in the Old Testament. A small part of a verse in the New Testament, may refer to a complete teaching in the Old.

For example, how can we understand what Paul meant when he wrote that we are kings and priests forever after the order of Melchizedek, if we have never understood what the functions of an Old Testament priest were, or even who Melchizedek was? How can we understand our rights and privileges as covenant children of God, if we don't know what a covenant is?

Patterns for Living from the Old Testament is not a complete study of the Old Testament. It is not a complete study of any event or theme contained in the Old Testament. It is an introduction – a broad view – of the main events and themes.

Once we have a basic understanding of the times and teaching of the Old Testament, everything we read or hear fits into that elementary outline and the picture God has given us becomes more and more clear.

This study is excellent for personal or group studies, Bible Schools, Sunday Schools, and home groups. It is important that both the teacher and the students have copies of this manual in hand during the course of the study. (Quantity discounts are available.)

The best books are written in, underlined, meditated on, and digested. We have left space for your notes and comments. The format has been designed with a fast reference system for review and to assist you in finding areas again. The special format makes it possible for each person, once they have studied through this material, to teach the contents to others.

Paul wrote to Timothy:

> **And the things you have heard me say in the presence of many witnesses entrust to reliable men who will also be qualified to teach others. (2 Timothy 2:2b)**

This course is designed as a practical participation Bible course in the MINDS (Ministry Development System) format, which is a specially developed approach to programmed learning. This concept is designed for multiplication in the lives, the ministry and the future teaching of the students. Former students, by using this manual, can teach this course easily to others.

Table of Contents

Charts

Acknowledgment
*Without the powerful, accurate input of **Dr. Jack Tuls,***
Patterns for Living from the Old Testament
might never have been written.
It is with great appreciation that we acknowledge his
contribution to this manual.

The Books of the Old Testament

I. Law

Genesis
Exodus
Leviticus
Numbers
Deuteronomy

II. History

Joshua
Judges
Ruth
I, II Samuel
I,II Kings
I,II Chronicles
Ezra
Nehemiah
Esther

III. Poetry

Job
Psalms
Proverbs
Ecclesiastes
Song of Solomon

IV. Prophets (17)
Major Prophets (5)

Isaiah
Jeremaiah
Lamentaions
Ezekiel
Daniel

Minor Prophets (12)

Hosea
Joel
Amos
Obadiah
Jonah
Micah
Nahum
Habakkuk
Zepheniah
Haggai
Zechariah
Malachi

Lesson One

God's Word for Us Today

THE BIBLE – GOD'S WORD

Description

The Bible is God's Word to His people. Through these words, we have a revelation of who God is and His eternal purpose for mankind. From the first page to the last, it tells of God's dealings with His people.

Content

In the Bible, we find God's will, God's ways, directions, and instructions. We find the answers to every problem that comes into our lives. It is our light, our bread, and our life.

Harmony

On any given subject throughout the entire Bible, there is harmony. The prophecies of the coming Messiah and their fulfillment are wonderful examples. There are 330 prophecies of the coming Messiah in the Old Testament fulfilled in the New Testament.

Confirmation

Archaeology has confirmed the Bible to be true in many details. It is in harmony with true science.

Indestructibility

The Bible has been publicly burnt – outlawed – its possession has meant death – and yet it has been preserved in its entirety. Outlawed for all but the priests through the dark ages of mankind's history, it was the first item printed on the first printing press. Five of these Gutenberg Bibles are still in existence.

Proliferation

The Bible has been translated into over 1,000 languages and there are over 30 million copies printed each year. It is the best selling book in the world.

Relevancy

The Bible still changes the lives of those who read it, and it still produces miracles in the lives of those who believe it.

David wrote about God's Word.

Psalm 119:105 Your word is a lamp to my feet and a light to my path.

Isaiah wrote,

Isaiah 55:10,11 For as the rain comes down, and the snow from heaven, and do not return there, but water the earth, and make it bring forth and bud, that it may give seed to the sower and bread to the eater, so shall My word be that goes forth from My mouth; it shall not return to Me void, but it shall accomplish what I please, and it shall prosper in the thing for which I sent it.

Jesus said,

Matthew 4:4 But He answered and said, "It is written, `Man shall not live by bread alone, but by every word that proceeds from the mouth of God.'"

Is Profitable

Paul wrote to Timothy that all scripture is profitable in our lives.

2 Timothy 3:16,17 All Scripture is given by inspiration of God, and is profitable for doctrine, for reproof, for correction, for instruction in righteousness, that the man of God may be complete, thoroughly equipped for every good work.

It is profitable for:
- Learning of doctrine
- Reproof (identifies sin – how you went wrong)
- Correction (shows how to correct your way)
- Instruction in righteousness
- Our completion
- Equipping us for every good work

THE BIBLE – INSPIRED BY GOD

Forty men, thirty-one in the Old Testament and nine in the New, wrote the words of the Bible over a period of 1,500 years. Obviously, most of them didn't know one another and were from different historical times and yet, there is no conflict. This could only happen because the Bible was written by men under the inspiration of the Holy Spirit.

God Breathed

The apostle Paul wrote that all Scripture was given by inspiration.

2 Timothy 3:16A All Scripture is given by inspiration of God ...

The Greek word translated *"inspiration of God"* means *"divinely breathed in."* This is the only place in the Bible where it is used.

Just as God breathed His life into Adam, God the Son, the living Word, breathed His life into the Scriptures. The Word is alive because it contains the life of God Himself.

The apostle John explained this.

John 1:1 In the beginning was the Word, and the Word was with God, and the Word was God.

Confirmed By

The Bible is inspired by God not only in its subject matter, but in every word down to the smallest detail – every *"jot and tittle."* This is confirmed by the Prophet Jeremiah and the apostles Matthew and John.

➢ *Jeremiah*

Jeremiah reveals some of the process of inspiration when he wrote about his instructions from God.

Jeremiah 36:2 Take a scroll of a book and write on it all the words that I have spoken to you against Israel, against Judah, and against all the nations, from the day I spoke to you, from the days of Josiah even to this day.

The writers of Scriptures were to write on the scroll of a book all of the words that He spoke to them through the Holy Spirit. Therefore, every word in the original scriptures was directly inspired of God.

➢ *Matthew*

The apostle Matthew wrote,

Matthew 5:18 For assuredly, I say to you, till heaven and earth pass away, one jot or one tittle will by no means pass from the law till all is fulfilled.

➢ *John*

The apostle John wrote,

Revelation 1:19 Write the things which you have seen, and the things which are, and the things which will take place after this.

The writers of Scriptures were to write the truths which were revealed to them by the Holy Spirit. He inspired them to write each word of the things that they saw in the Spirit, about the things which existed at the time of the writing, and the things that He revealed to them which were to take place in the future.

The process of inspiration came as thoughts that were expressed in exact words given through supernatural visions and revelations. While using the personalities of the human authors, every Word of the original Scriptures was inspired (or breathed) through the supernatural work of the Holy Spirit.

THE BIBLE'S ABSOLUTE INFALLIBILITY

The infallibility of all Scripture is revealed in the Word by referring to the trustworthiness of the Word of God.

Apostle Peter

The Word of God is called *"more sure"* than even the great experience that Peter had while on the Mount of Transfiguration with Jesus. After describing this great experience, he went on to write,

2 Peter 1:19 We also have the prophetic word made more sure, which you do well to heed as a light that shines in a dark place.

Dr. Luke

The certainty of Scripture was attested to by Luke. He began his gospel account by writing about the word that was delivered to him. He continues by saying that these things were written *that you may know the certainty of those things in which you were instructed* (Luke 1:4).

Apostle John

John wrote regarding the absolute truth of all Scripture.

John 19:35 And he who has seen has testified, and his testimony is true; and he knows that he is telling the truth, so that you may believe.

Apostle Paul

The Scriptures are worthy of our acceptance.

1 Timothy 4:9 This is a faithful saying and worthy of all acceptance.

THE BIBLE'S ABSOLUTE AUTHORITY

Knowing Right from Wrong

Contrary to the teaching of modern philosophy, there are absolute truths, values, ethics and authority in the universe. These absolutes are revealed in the Word of God.

It is through these absolutes that we can know right from wrong. The Bible is the only absolute authority for our lives.

Psalm 119:11 Your word I have hidden in my heart, that I might not sin against You.

Only True Gospel

There is no other true gospel than the one revealed in God's Word.

Galatians 1:8 But even if we, or an angel from heaven, preach any other gospel to you than what we have preached to you, let him be accursed.

Absolute Authority

God's Word is absolute authority because it is absolute truth.

Jesus said,

John 17:17 Sanctify them by Your truth. Your word is truth.

Demands Obedience

The absolute authority of God's Word demands our obedience.

2 Thessalonians 3:14 And if anyone does not obey our word in this epistle, note that person and do not keep company with him, that he may be ashamed.

Because of the absolute authority of God's Word, we can only be blessed as we read, hear, and keep its truths.

Joshua 1:8 This Book of the law shall not depart from your mouth, but you shall meditate in it day and night, that you may observe to do according to all that is written in it. For then you will make your way prosperous, and then you will have good success.

THE CANON OF SCRIPTURE

The *"Canon of Scripture"* refers to those books which were selected by learned men who, after much prayer and study, determined, as they were led by the Holy Spirit, that God's total and complete written revelation to His people was contained in, and limited to only sixty-six books.

They used several tests to decide if a book was to be part of the New Testament.

> ➢ Written by an apostle or one close to an apostle
> ➢ Widely read
> ➢ Accepted for life and doctrine
> ➢ Used in public worship
> ➢ Church-wide acceptance
> ➢ Approved by decision of the whole church

Over a period of 1,500 years, forty men wrote the Bible. There are no contradictions because there was actually only one source, the Holy Spirit. Each person wrote as he was inspired by the same Holy Spirit.

Some may ask, *"How do we know that other books shouldn't have been included as a part of the Scriptures?"*

The answer is found in the fact that all of the Scriptures have but one major theme – the revelation of Jesus Christ as the Savior of sinful mankind.

The Old Testament's prophecies, promises, sacrifices, and worship all point forward to Jesus. The New Testament gives us the story of His life on this earth, and points back to what He purchased for us with His death on Calvary, and tells us what to expect in the future.

Jesus endorsed twenty-three of the books of the Old Testament in His teaching.

The Apocrypha

There were other books written during the period of our Old Testament. During the first century, biblical scholars studied these works, and they came into agreement that many of these books weren't inspired by God.

Some of these books were later accepted by the Catholic Church of Rome and became part of their Bible. These books are called the Apocrypha.

Apocrypha in Greek means *"hidden"* or *"secret."* This name could have been chosen since the author, date of writing, and origin of these books is very doubtful. Some of these books give conflicting accounts and doctrines to those books which were carefully selected as the inspired Word of God.

Most were rejected because they were of a different spirit, a different anointing, and contained points that were considered error when compared to the other books of Scripture.

While these books contain interesting historical information, we must be careful not to accept them with the same absolute authority as we do the recognized Scriptures.

Note: For more information on this subject we suggest you read the book, **All About the Bible**, by Sidney Collett published by Fleming H. Revell.

Extra-Biblical Revelations

Historical
1 & 2 Esdras
1 & 2 Maccabees
Additions to Daniel
Additionas to Esther
Epistle to Jeremy
Prayer of Manasseh

Legendary
Baruch
Tobit
Judith

Apocalyptic
Fourth Esdras

Didactic
Wisdom of Solomon
Sirach (Ecclesiasticus)

Dreams, visions, prophecies, and angelic appearances are all valid today. However, none of them can be given the same authority as the Word of God. We are warned in Scripture not to add to or change what the Bible teaches. There is a strong danger in anyone adding *"details"* to God's Word by prophecy, visions, etc.

Revelation 22:18,19 For I testify to everyone who hears the words of the prophecy of this book: if anyone adds to these things, God will add to him the plagues that are written in this book. And if anyone takes away from the words of the book of this prophecy, God will take away his part from the Book of Life, from the holy city, and from the things which are written in this book.

Most deception, false doctrine, cults, and false religions contain large elements of truth. These truths are then mixed with satanic deception. Through the gift of the discerning of spirits, we can distinguish truth from error.

Original Languages

The Bible was originally written in three languages. The Old Testament was written mainly in Hebrew. Parts of Daniel and Nehemiah were written in Aramaic. The New Testament was written in Greek.

Translations

Over the years, the Bible has been translated into many languages. There are many different translations of the Bible in the English language. In a basic translation, the scholars have gone back to the original languages and expressed the word-by-word meaning of the words from the ancient texts.

Because the original Hebrew and Greek languages have exact and distinct meanings for each word, the job of the translator has been to carefully select the word in our

English language that would best convey the meaning of the original. However, since the English language is not as exact a language as the original, some of the full rich meaning of the original has been missed.

The Amplified Bible and other expanded translations have attempted to overcome this challenge, and are excellent study Bibles. By their very nature, they are somewhat wordy and are not as easy to read.

Paraphrase

Sometimes, the scholars didn't try to translate the Bible word-for-word; instead, they paraphrased it. This means they translated it thought-by-thought. These versions are easier to understand because they flow more easily in our language and are great for devotional reading.

For Bible study, it is better to use a basic translation which tends to be more accurate. For this study, we are using the New King James Version of the Bible.

BOOK OF COVENANTS

Before we enter into a study of some of the main themes of the Old Testament, it's important to understand some basic truths about the whole Bible. The word *"Bible"* means *"the books."*

The Bible is divided into two main sections, and these are called the Old and New Testaments.

Definition

A testament is a covenant. A covenant is a serious binding agreement between two or more parties. The Bible contains the covenants that God made with His people.

The Old Testament contains the Old Covenants God made with mankind before the coming of Christ. It looks forward to the completed work of Christ. The New Testament contains the New Covenant and is based on the completed work of Christ on this earth.

Old Testament
➤ *Prophets*

Since sixteen books of the Old Testament were written by prophets, it is important to understand the prophet's function.

➤ They spoke the Word of God to the people.
➤ They were God's spokesmen to the kings and people of Israel and Judah.
➤ They warned against sin and prophesied judgment.
➤ They can be compared to the plumb line mentioned in Amos which was used by builders to keep the corner of the building straight as it was being built.

The prophets were different from the priests in that they spoke for God to mankind. The priests spoke to God for mankind.

➤ *Thirty-Nine Books*

There are thirty-nine books in the Old Testament.

The books of the Old Testament are not arranged in chronological order. Instead they are arranged by category. For example, the books of poetry are arranged together even though most scholars agree that Job is the oldest book in the Bible.

➤ *Importance*

There are people who say the Old Testament isn't really important to study. But if we ignore it, we are ignoring two-thirds of what God has said to us! The Old Testament isn't *"just a history of the Jewish race,"* it is a pattern for our lives and ministries.

It provides the foundation to understand God's creative purpose for our lives. It provides the foundation to understand God's great love-plan of redemption. It reveals God's plan and purpose to restore us to be, have, and do all that was in His heart when He created us in His image.

In this study, we'll focus our attention on some major truths that are revealed in the Old Testament. It would be impossible in one manual to study all of the rich, wonderful things God did for His people, all the wonderful things He taught, or all the wonderful things He has promised us through these pages.

This study will be a beginning. It is an introduction to the Old Testament, a brief over-all outline into which you'll be adding revelation the rest of your life!

What God said to Adam and Eve is still in effect. What God promised Abraham is still in effect. The people of Old Testament times had their needs met by looking, in faith, forward to what the Messiah was going to establish for them. As believers today, we look back, in faith, to what Christ has done for us.

QUESTIONS FOR REVIEW

1. What is meant by the phrase in 2 Timothy 3:16, *"All Scripture is given by inspiration of God"?* Describe the process of biblical inspiration.

2. What is meant by the terms *"the infallibility of all Scripture"* and *"the absolute authority of Scripture"?* Give scriptural references that provide a foundation for these truths.

3. What is meant by the phrase *"Canon of Scripture"?* Describe why the Scriptures are limited to only sixty-six books.

Lesson Two

Main Events of the Old Testament Period

In this lesson, we'll cover 3,600 years of history. Of necessity, some of the most profound events will be covered in one or two paragraphs. This is to establish an overview or outline, into which all the other lessons will fit.

When tackling a large volume of information, it makes it easier to understand if we divide it into *"digestible"* sections. The Old Testament covers about 3,600 years, and can be divided into nine periods.

➢ Creation to the Flood – 4,000 to 2,350 B.C.
➢ Age of the Patriarchs – 2,350 to 1,840 B.C.
➢ Children of Israel in Egypt – 1,840 to 1,440 B.C.
➢ From Egypt to Canaan – 1,440 to 1,400 B.C.
➢ Period of Judges – 1,400 to 1,051 B.C.
➢ Establishing Kingdom of Israel – 1,051 to 931 B.C.
➢ Kingdom Divided – Captivity- 931 to 586 B.C.
➢ Babylonian Captivity – 605 to 535 B.C.
➢ The Restoration – 535 to 400 B.C.

FROM CREATION TO FLOOD

4,000 to 2,350 B.C.

Creation

Genesis is the book of beginnings. We are given the begining of:

➢ The world
➢ The human race
➢ God's relationship with man
➢ Sin
➢ The promises of a coming Redeemer
➢ Death
➢ Different languages
➢ The Jewish nation
➢ God's revelation of Himself

Sin Enters the Human Race

God created the earth and everything on the earth, and then He created Adam and Eve. They were His crowning creations. They were:

➢ Created in His image
➢ Created to have dominion over all creation
➢ Created to have a glorious destiny
➢ Created to have a relationship with God
➢ Created to have communion with God

God placed them in the Garden of Eden and told them they could eat of everything in the garden except the fruit of one tree. God established that mankind's relationship to Him would be one of obedience.

We know what happened. Eve and then Adam rebelled against what God had said. They ate fruit from that tree, and their rebellion brought:

➢ Alienation from God
➢ Fear of His Presence
➢ Blaming others
➢ Loss of dominion over creation
➢ Loss of the image and glory of God
➢ Toil
➢ Death

First Sacrifice

God made coats of skins to cover Adam and Eve and this was the first death of an animal – the first sacrifice made on behalf of mankind.

First Promise of Redeemer

As God was pronouncing the curses that came as a result of their sin, He didn't leave them without hope. He gave them a wonderful promise concerning the Seed of the woman.

Genesis 3:15 And I will put enmity between you and the woman, and between your seed and her Seed; He shall bruise your head, and you shall bruise His heel.

First Murder

In Genesis 4, we read of the birth of Cain and Abel, of the sacrifices they made, of jealousy and of the first murder. Cain slew Abel.

From the time of Adam and Eve's sin, things grew worse until the thoughts of mankind were evil continually.

Genesis 6:5 Then the LORD saw that the wickedness of man was great in the earth, and that every intent of the thoughts of his heart was only evil continually.

The Flood

In every age, God has a remnant of believers. Even during the horrible, evil time before the flood, Enoch, wa*lked with God and then was not for God took him.*

Noah was a righteous man, whom God could tell to build an ark for the preservation of the human race, and of the animals and birds.

Even after God's judgement and the destruction of everything on the earth, men and women didn't obey God.

Tower of Babel

God instructed the people to be fruitful, to multiply, and replenish the earth. But instead, they gathered in the land of Shinar. They decided to stay there and not to scatter over the face of the earth – not to replenish the earth.

Genesis 11:4 And they said, "Come, let us build ourselves a city, and a tower whose top is in the heavens; let us make a name for ourselves, lest we be scattered abroad over the face of the whole earth."

They were in rebellion against God.

Genesis 11:6-8 And the LORD said, "Indeed the people are one and they all have one language, and this is what they begin to do; now nothing that they propose to do will be withheld from them. Come, let Us go down and there confuse their language, that they may not understand one another's speech."

So the LORD scattered them abroad from there over the face of all the earth, and they ceased building the city.

It is important to note that God said that with unity of purpose and a common language, mankind could do anything.

AGE OF PATRIARCHS

2,350 to 1,840 B.C.

The title of patriarch was given in the New Testament to those who founded the Hebrew race and nation before the time of Moses. In the Age of Patriarchs, the ruler of a clan was the oldest male. The patriarchal head was also the priest of his household.

Job

Job is the oldest book of the Bible and as such is the first example of a patriarch. The love of a father and the priesthood of the head of the family is made clear when we read:

Job 1:5 So it was, when the days of feasting had run their course, that Job would send and sanctify them, and he would rise early in the morning and offer burnt offerings according to the number of them all. For Job said, "It may be that my sons have sinned and cursed God in their hearts." Thus Job did regularly.

The book of Job tells us about Job losing his family, and his health. But through it all he proclaimed:

Job 19:23-26 Oh, that my words were written! Oh, that they were inscribed in a book! That they were engraved on a rock with an iron pen and lead, forever! For I know that my Redeemer lives, and He shall stand at last on the earth; and after my skin is destroyed, this I know, that in my flesh I shall see God ...

Abraham and Isaac

Abraham is the next example of a patriarch. God called him out of Ur to re-establish the eternal covenant with mankind, and to establish the nation of Israel.

The promised son of Abraham was Isaac. Isaac means the laughing one, and his birth brought laughter to both Abraham and Sarah.

Isaac had two sons, Esau and Jacob. Esau, though he was the oldest, sold his birthright to Jacob. The Bible says he despised his birthright. In reality, Esau cared more about the things of this earth than the privilege of being the head, or the priest of his family.

Jacob (Israel)

Jacob was the younger son of Isaac who through deception obtained the birthright and became part of the promised line. His life started out as one of deceit, but he met God and his life was changed. God changed his name to Israel which means ruler as God. Israel had twelve sons and the descendants of these sons became the twelve tribes of Israel.

Joseph

Joseph was the favored son of Israel, but his jealous brothers sold him into slavery. As a slave he was falsely accused and put in prison, but from there God raised him up to be next to Pharaoh. Joseph prospered wherever he was.

When Joseph was reunited with his brothers and Jacob, all their families (seventy people) moved to Egypt. They moved into an honored position, but over a period of time this changed.

Exodus 1:6-9 And Joseph died, all his brothers, and all that generation. But the children of Israel were fruitful and increased abundantly, multiplied and grew exceedingly mighty; and the land was filled with them. Now there arose a new king over Egypt, who didn't know Joseph. And he said to his people, "Look, the people of the children of Israel are more and mightier than we."

CHILDREN OF ISRAEL IN EGYPT

1,840 to 1,440 B.C.

God's blessings were on the children of Israel and the more they were persecuted, the more they grew in number.

Exodus 1:12-14a But the more they afflicted them, the more they multiplied and grew. And they were in dread of the children of Israel. So the Egyptians made the children of Israel serve with rigor. And they made their lives bitter with hard bondage.

Moses

To lessen the number of the children of Israel, Pharaoh commanded that all the boys that were born be cast into the river. When Moses was born, his mother hid him for three months. Then, because she couldn't keep him hidden any longer, she took a basket and made it as waterproof as possible. She placed Moses in the basket and placed it in the river.

God had His hand on Moses. The daughter of Pharaoh found the baby and hired his own mother to nurse and care for him.

Moses was raised as the son of Pharaoh's daughter. And yet, at the age of forty when he saw an Egyptian beating a Hebrew slave, he killed the Egyptian. He identified with his people, and was forced to flee for his life.

Moses lived in Midian as a sheepherder for the next forty years. And then, one day he stopped to investigate a bush that was on fire, but didn't burn. God spoke to him and called him to deliver His people from Egypt.

Ten Plagues

When God sent Moses to ask Pharaoh to let the children of Israel go, he refused. (The Pharaoh of Moses' childhood had died.) God sent ten plagues on the Epyptians before Pharaoh was willing to let them leave.

➢ The Nile River, which they worshiped as a god, turned to blood.

➢ Frogs by the thousands came out of the river and were everywhere.

➢ The dust of the land became lice.

➢ Swarms of flies came upon everything.

➢ A severe plague causing death came on their cattle, horses, asses, camels, oxen, and sheep.

➢ Both the people and the animals that were left, broke out in severe boils.

➢ Hail came in such force that any person or animal left outside died.

➢ So many locusts came that the earth couldn't be seen. They ate everything, even the trees.

➢ A thick darkness covered the earth for three days. It was a darkness so intense it could be felt.

After each plague, Pharaoh was given an opportunity to obey God, but he refused.

➢ The final plague was the death of the firstborn of both the Egyptians and the Israelites.

God had given specific instructions for the Israelites for this night. They were to make a sacrifice and apply the blood to the doorposts. They were to eat the sacrifice dressed for travel. The firstborn of the Israelites who didn't apply the blood to the doorpost – those who didn't obey God – died along with the firstborn of the Egyptians. This was the first Passover feast and it was fulfilled when Jesus was sacrificed on the cross providing the blood covering for our salvation.

Exodus 12:13 Now the blood shall be a sign for you on the houses where you are. And when I see the blood, I will pass over you; and the plague shall not be on you to destroy you when I strike the land of Egypt.

FROM EGYPT TO CANAAN

1,440 to 1,400 B.C.

Parting of Red Sea

The seventy people who had moved to Egypt had become a mighty multitude. After the death of the firstborn, Pharaoh "thrust them out" of the land. But then, he changed his mind and sent his army to bring them back.

The Israelites were caught. There were mountains to the sides, the Red Sea in front, and Pharaoh's army behind. God set a pillar of cloud and fire between them and the army, to protect them . On the Israelite's side it was light, but on the Egyptian's side it was dark. Then God parted the Red Sea and the multitude crossed on dry ground.

When the Egyptian army tried to follow, the waters hurled down on them and they drowned.

Giving of Law

God led the people to Mount Sinai and there they sanctified themselves for three days. Exactly fifty days after they left Egypt, after the first Passover, the law was given. Fifty days after Jesus left this earth, the Holy Spirit came to write the law on our hearts.

Exodus 19:16-20 Then it came to pass on the third day, in the morning, that there were thunderings and lightnings, and a thick cloud on the mountain; and the sound of the trumpet was very loud, so that all the people who were in the camp trembled.

And Moses brought the people out of the camp to meet with God, and they stood at the foot of the mountain.

Now Mount Sinai was completely in smoke, because the LORD descended upon it in fire. Its smoke ascended like the smoke of a furnace, and the whole mountain quaked greatly. And when the blast of the trumpet sounded long and became louder and louder, Moses spoke, and God answered him by voice.

Then the LORD came down upon Mount Sinai, on the top of the mountain. And the LORD called Moses to the top of the mountain, and Moses went up.

Golden Calf

While Moses was talking with the Lord – even though they had seen the wonderful things He had done, even though they heard His voice in the thundering – while the Lord was giving the law and the plans for the tabernacle to Moses, the people, with the help of Aaron, made a golden calf and worshiped it.

God said to Moses, *I'll destroy these people, and make of you a great nation.* But Moses interceded for them and God forgave them.

The children of Israel came to the borders of Canaan, but they refused to believe God could bring them victory in the land, and they wandered in the wilderness for forty years.

PERIOD OF THE JUDGES – TAKING THE LAND

1,400 to 1,051 B.C.

Moses had died and been buried by God on Mount Horeb. Joshua had taken over the leadership of the children of Israel when, forty years later, they came again to the border of Canaan.

Again, God dried up the waters of a river. This time it was the Jordan River, and the people walked across on dry ground. The walls of Jericho supernaturally fell, and they began the conquest of the land of Canaan.

Canaan was divided with each of the tribes having their own land, except the tribe of Levi, the priestly tribe.

The nation of Israel was different from the surrounding nations in that they didn't have a human king. God was their king. Following the leadership of Joshua, they had judges to govern them. The principal judges were:
- Othniel – the first judge
- Deborah – a woman
- Gideon – the mighty man of valor
- Jephthah
- Samson – the strong man
- Eli
- Samuel – the last judge.

ESTABLISHING KINGDOM OF ISRAEL

1,051 to 931 B.C.

People Demand a King

When Samuel was an old man, the people demanded a king. They rebelled from being ruled by God, and God let them have their own way. Listen to the warning He gave them.

1 Samuel 8:7 And the LORD said to Samuel, "Heed the voice of the people in all that they say to you; for they have not rejected you, but they have rejected Me, that I should not reign over them."

He warned them that a king would take:
- Their sons for himself
- Their daughters for himself
- Their fields, vineyards, and olive yards and give them to others
- A tenth of everything they had

God continued His warning,

1 Samuel 8:18,19 "And you will cry out in that day because of your king whom you have chosen for yourselves, and the LORD will not hear you in that day."

Nevertheless the people refused to obey the voice of Samuel; and they said, "No, but we will have a king over us."

God gave them what they demanded even though it was not good for them. Samuel anointed Saul to be king. From being a theocracy, a nation ruled by God, they became a monarchy, a nation ruled by man.

Saul

Saul started out anointed by God. He was humble and practiced self-control, but he grew to be proud and disobedient. Finally, God said to Samuel,

1 Samuel 15:10,11 Now the word of the LORD came to Samuel, saying, "I greatly regret that I have set up Saul as king, for he has turned back from following Me, and has not performed My commandments."

Samuel had tried to warn Saul but he refused to listen. Then God sent Samuel to anoint the next king.

Saul ended his life by having his servant kill him.

David

David was the second king of Israel, and the nation became the strongest and largest in size during his reign. God said David was a man after His own heart.

1 Samuel 13:14b The LORD has sought for Himself a man after His own heart, and the LORD has commanded him to be commander over His people, because you have not kept what the LORD commanded you.

David was a warrior, a king, a prophet, and a psalmist. God gave to him the plans for the temple.

David wrote much of the book of Psalms and taught people how to praise and worship God.

Most of David's reign was a testimony to God, but he had two areas of weakness – women, and failing to discipline those close to him. In his ending years, his sons were rebellious, caused a lot of strife, and even tried to steal his kingdom.

Solomon

Solomon began his reign with great favor. He was anointed king with David's blessings. He had immense stores of wealth collected by his father. He was loved and accepted with high hopes by the people.

His greatest desire, as he began to rule, was for wisdom, and he was given divinely imparted mental abilities. It is believed that he collected and wrote the book of Proverbs, the Song of Solomon, and the book of Ecclesiastes in his later years.

He built the great temple of God. And yet, Solomon fell into carnality and idolatry. He had seven hundred wives and three hundred concubines. Perhaps the book of Ecclesiastes is a picture of himself in the later years.

KINGDOM DIVIDED – FALLS INTO CAPTIVITY

931 to 586 B.C.

At Solomon's death, Rehoboam became the king of Israel. The people asked him to ease their heavy tax burden. Rehoboam went to the older men and they said that if he was kind to the people, pleased them, and spoke good words to them, they would be his servants forever.

He refused their counsel and went to the young men he had grown up with. They said to tell the people:

1 Kings 12:11 " 'And now, whereas my father laid a heavy yoke on you, I will add to your yoke; my father chastised you with whips, but I will chastise you with scourges!' "

The people of the northern tribes rebelled and the nation of Israel was divided.

Israel – The Northern Kingdom

The Northern Kingdom was made up of ten tribes. It was a nation born in rebellion. There were nineteen different kings, but not one was a good king.

Ahab was the evil king of Elijah's time and Jezebel was his wife.

Jehoram, Jehu, Jehoahaz, and Jehoash were the evil kings of Elisha's time.

The prophets, Hosea, Amos, Elijah, and Elisha warned the kings and people of this kingdom. Jonah was also from this kingdom.

In Second Kings seventeen, we are given a list of the terrible sins of the northern kingdom. Finally, their sins were so great that God let them go into captivity.

Judah – The Southern Kingdom

The Southern Kingdom was made up of two tribes.

Out of twenty kings, they had eight good kings, and God spared Judah longer because of these kings.

Some of the good kings were Jehoshaphat who restored order in worship, Joash, Uzziah, Jotham and Hezekiah. The prophets of Judah were Micah, Habakkuk, Joel, Jeremiah, Obadiah, Isaiah, Nahum, and Zephaniah.

The book of Lamentations is an expression of Jeremiah's sorrow over the fall of Judah. It ends with these words:

Lamentations 5:21 Turn us back to You, O LORD, and we will be restored ...

BABYLONIAN CAPTIVITY

605 to 535 B.C.

One of the most comforting things we can learn from the Old Testament is that God controls nations. They rise to power and they fall according to His plans. The children of Israel were disobedient and worshiped other gods and God raised the nation of Babylon to discipline and enslave them.

One of the captains of the Babylonian army knew why the people of Judah had fallen.

Jeremiah 40:2,3 And the captain of the guard took Jeremiah and said to him: "The LORD your God has pronounced this doom on this place. Now the LORD has brought it, and has done just as He said. Because you people have sinned against the LORD, and not obeyed His voice, therefore this thing has come upon you."

Nebuchadnezzar

The people of Judah were not all taken at one time into captivity. Daniel, Shadrach, Meshach and Abednego were in the first group to be taken and they moved into positions of leadership. Nebuchadnezzar was the king of Babylon. It was during his reign that Shadrach, Meshach and Abednego were thrown into the fiery furnace and came out alive. Nebuchadnezzar became full of pride and took credit for all the things God had given him.

Daniel 4:30 The king spoke, saying, "Is not this great Babylon, that I have built for a royal dwelling by my mighty power and for the honor of my majesty?"

At that moment he went insane and lived in the field as an animal. Daniel had warned him this would happen and that he would stay in this condition for seven years until he would:

know that the Most High rules in the kingdom of men, and gives it to whomever He chooses (Daniel 4:25b).

At the end of seven years, Nebuchadnezzar came back to his right mind, and he said,

Daniel 4:37 Now I, Nebuchadnezzar, praise and extol and honor the King of heaven, all of whose works are truth, and His ways justice. And those who walk in pride He is able to abase.

Belshazzar

Belshazzar, the grandson of Nebuchadnezzar, was the last king of Babylon. We know almost nothing about him except that at his last great feast, there were thousands in attendance drinking from the silver and gold vessels taken from the temple in Jerusalem. A hand appeared and wrote a message on the wall which Daniel interpreted.

Daniel 5:26-28,31 "This is the interpretation of each word. Mene: God has numbered your kingdom, and finished it; Tekel: You have been weighed in the balances, and found wanting; Peres: Your kingdom has been divided, and given to the Medes and Persians."

Daniel 5:30,31a That very night Belshazzar, king of the Chaldeans, was slain. And Darius the Mede received the kingdom.

Israel had become evil and fell to the Babylonians. Babylon became evil and fell to the Persians.

Cyrus

Cyrus was the founder of the Persian Empire, he conquered Babylon and was anointed by God to free the Jews from captivity. The prophet, Isaiah, foretold the coming of Cyrus, and mentioned him by name two hundred years before Cyrus was born.

Isaiah 44:24a,28 Thus says the LORD, your Redeemer ... Who says of Cyrus, `He is My shepherd, and he shall perform all My pleasure, even saying to Jerusalem, "You shall be built," and to the temple, "Your foundation shall be laid." '

THE RESTORATION

535 to 400 B.C.

The people returned to Israel at three different times. The first to return were Zerubbabel, Jeshua, Haggai, and Zechariah. Their purpose was to rebuild the temple.

Ezra was in the second group and his purpose was to restore the teaching of the law and righteous worship.

Finally Nehemiah and the others returned to rebuild the walls of Jerusalem.

The date of the writing of the book of Malachi is not certain. It may be that it is actually the last book to be written in the Old Testament. Malachi wrote,

Malachi 4:2a "But to you who fear My name the Sun of Righteousness shall arise with healing in His wings ..."

QUESTIONS FOR REVIEW

1. What are the nine periods of Old Testament history that are listed in this lesson?

2. What warning did God give the people of Israel when they desired to be like the other nations and asked for a human king?

3. According to this lesson, what is one of the most comforting things that we can learn from the Old Testament? Give biblical examples of this truth.

Lesson Three
Covenant Children of God

Introduction

Before God created the earth, He planned the creation of mankind. He knew, through His foreknowledge, that Adam and Eve were going to sin, and He planned the coming of a Redeemer. God is a:

➤ Covenant-making,
➤ Covenant-keeping,
➤ Covenant-revealing God.
➤ Moses wrote about this.

Deuteronomy 7:9 Therefore know that the LORD your God, He is God, the faithful God who keeps covenant and mercy for a thousand generations with those who love Him and keep His commandments.

Before creation, God established an Everlasting Covenant with mankind. This covenant is still in effect. This covenant belongs to us!

The covenants of God established in the Old Testament are still part of our lives today.

Definition

A covenant is a serious, binding agreement, a contract, between God and His people. A blood covenant is a covenant sealed by His own blood which cannot be broken.

God was the initiator of these covenants, and He presented them to mankind as a progressive revelation of Himself, His plans, and His purposes.

Two Types
➤ *Unconditional*

There are two types of covenants – unconditional and conditional. An unconditional covenant is an obligation undertaken by God, on mankind's behalf. These will be fulfilled regardless of obedience or disobedience.

➤ *Conditional*

Other covenants are conditional covenants and can either be accepted or rejected by mankind. The conditions of these covenants are set by God, who is unchangeable. Therefore the conditions cannot be changed. The benefits of a conditional covenant can only be received through faith and obedience.

EVERLASTING COVENANT (Conditional)

A Foundational Covenant

The Everlasting Covenant began in eternity past in the counsel of God the Father, Son and Holy Spirit. God planned the creation of mankind to fulfill His desire for an eternal family. He desired a bride for His Son and an everlasting family through which He could duplicate Himself.

Foreknowing the rebellion and fall of Adam and Eve, He planned their redemption through the death of His Son. Through redemption, mankind was to be restored to all that they were created to be. Men and women would be perfect, righteous, completed, a fitting, everlasting bride for His Son.

It is this foundational eternal covenant on which all the covenants in time are based.

We Are
➢ *Called*

The Everlasting Covenant reveals God's purpose and grace toward mankind.

2 Timothy 1:9,10 Who has saved us and called us with a holy calling, not according to our works, but according to His own purpose and grace which was given to us in Christ Jesus before time began, but has now been revealed by the appearing of our Savior Jesus Christ, who has abolished death and brought life and immortality to light through the gospel.

➢ *Redeemed*

It reveals God's redemptive plan for mankind through the shedding of the blood of His Son.

Hebrews 13:20 Now may the God of peace who brought up our LORD Jesus from the dead, that great Shepherd of the sheep, through the blood of the Everlasting Covenant ...

➢ *Predestined in Christ*

It reveals God's plan that mankind would be created and later conformed to the image of His Son.

Romans 8:29,30 For whom He foreknew, He also predestined to be conformed to the image of His Son, that He might be the firstborn among many brethren. Moreover whom He predestined, these He also called; whom He called, these He also justified; and whom He justified, these He also glorified.

➢ *With a Future*

God's Eternal Covenant with mankind from eternity past established our future.

Ephesians 1:4 Just as He chose us in Him before the foundation of the world, that we should be holy and without blame before Him in love ...

Patterns for Living

1 Corinthians 2:7 But we speak the wisdom of God in a mystery, the hidden wisdom which God ordained before the ages for our glory.

Our Blessings

➢ *Eternal Life*

As participants in the Everlasting Covenant, we have eternal life. It is God's life within us.

Titus 1:2 In hope of eternal life which God, who cannot lie, promised before time began ...

➢ *His Love*

We can receive His love.

Jeremiah 31:3 The LORD has appeared of old to me, saying: "Yes, I have loved you with an everlasting love; therefore with lovingkindness I have drawn you."

➢ *Righteousness*

According to Daniel 9:24,

God purposes were to make an end of sins, to make reconciliation for iniquity, to bring in everlasting righteousness ...

The redemptive work of Christ on our behalf was to bring reconciliation for iniquity, and to bring everlasting righteousness.

2 Corinthians 5:21 He made Him who knew no sin to be sin for us, that we might become the righteousness of God in Him.

➢ *Name*

We are given an everlasting name.

Isaiah 56:5 Even to them I will give in My house and within My walls a place and a name better than that of sons and daughters; I will give them an everlasting name that shall not be cut off.

➢ *Kingdom*

We became part of an everlasting kingdom.

Daniel 7:27 Then the kingdom and dominion, and the greatness of the kingdoms under the whole heaven, shall be given to the people, the saints of the Most High. His kingdom is an everlasting kingdom, and all dominions shall serve and obey Him.

➢ *Everlasting Joy*

We have everlasting joy.

Isaiah 51:11 So the ransomed of the LORD shall return, and come to Zion with singing, with everlasting joy on their heads; they shall obtain joy and gladness, and sorrow and sighing shall flee away.

The Conditions

God's part was to provide all the blessings of the covenant. What is our part? What are the conditions to receive the everlasting covenant and make it ours, both for now and all eternity?

➤ *Believing Faith*

There is only one way to receive this Everlasting Covenant into our lives – by believing faith.

John 3:16 For God so loved the world that He gave His only begotten Son, that whoever believes in Him should not perish but have everlasting life.

➤ *Obedience*

The way we keep the eternal covenant effective in our lives is through obedience.

John 14:15 If you love Me, keep My commandments.

Hebrews 5:9 And having been perfected, He became the author of eternal salvation to all who obey Him ...

➤ *Sealed*

Even as the Everlasting Covenant was planned by the Father and executed by the Son, the Everlasting Covenant is sealed by the Holy Spirit.

Ephesians 1:13 In Him you also trusted, after you heard the word of truth, the gospel of your salvation; in whom also, having believed, you were sealed with the Holy Spirit of promise ...

EDENIC COVENANT (Conditional)

The Edenic Covenant was the first covenant God established when He created Adam and Eve and placed them in the Garden of Eden. In it, He revealed His purpose and plan for humanity.

This covenant, as all the others, provided both a blessing for obedience and a curse for disobedience.

The Blessings

Genesis 1:28-30 Then God blessed them, and God said to them, "Be fruitful and multiply; fill the earth and subdue it; have dominion over the fish of the sea, over the birds of the air, and over every living thing that moves on the earth."

And God said, "See, I have given you every herb that yields seed which is on the face of all the earth, and every tree whose fruit yields seed; to you it shall be for food. Also, to every beast of the earth, to every bird of the air, and to everything that creeps on the earth, in which there is life, I have given every green herb for food"; and it was so.

The Conditions

Just as there was a blessing for obedience, a test of that obedience was provided by God. If Adam and Eve disobeyed, they would receive the curse of the covenant.

Genesis 2:16,17 And the LORD God commanded the man, saying, "Of every tree of the garden you may freely eat; but of the tree of the knowledge of good and evil you shall not eat, for in the day that you eat of it you shall surely die."

The Edenic Covenant put Adam and Eve on probation to test their commitment to the terms of the covenant.

Covenant Broken

After Adam and Eve ate the fruit, their fellowship with God was broken. They could no longer come boldly into the presence of God.

Genesis 3:8 And they heard the sound of the LORD God walking in the garden in the cool of the day, and Adam and his wife hid themselves from the presence of the LORD God among the trees of the garden.

➢ *Curse on Satan*

Because of Satan's part in the fall of mankind, a curse was put on him.

Genesis 3:14,15 So the LORD God said to the serpent: "Because you have done this, you are cursed more than all cattle, and more than every beast of the field; on your belly you shall go, and you shall eat dust all the days of your life. And I will put enmity between you and the woman, and between your seed and her Seed; He shall bruise your head, and you shall bruise His heel."

➢ *Curse on Eve*

A curse was put on women.

Genesis 3:16 To the woman He said: "I will greatly multiply your sorrow and your conception; in pain you shall bring forth children; your desire shall be for your husband, and he shall rule over you."

➢ *Curse on Adam and Ground*

The curse put on Adam, and thus all men, included a curse on the ground. From this day on, he would be forced to work all the days of his life, and he would sweat while doing it. It would be hard and unpleasant.

Genesis 3:17,18 Then to Adam He said, "Because you have heeded the voice of your wife, and have eaten from the tree of which I commanded you, saying, `You shall not eat of it.' Cursed is the ground for your sake; in toil you shall eat of it all the days of your life. Both thorns and thistles it shall bring forth for you, and you shall eat the herb of the field.

Instead of producing good things only, the ground would bring forth thorns and thistles.

➢ *Death*

Death came on all creation, and on mankind.

Genesis 3:19 In the sweat of your face you shall eat bread till you return to the ground, for out of it you were taken; for dust you are, and to dust you shall return."

➢ *Jesus Became Our Curse*

We must never stop with a listing of the curses that came as a result of sin, without remembering that Jesus, through His suffering and death on the cross, became our curse.

Galatians 3:13 Christ has redeemed us from the curse of the law, having become a curse for us (for it is written, "Cursed is everyone who hangs on a tree.")

ADAMIC COVENANT (Unconditional)

Even in the midst of the curses which came on Adam and Eve through their sins, God gave them a promise of redemption. God made a new covenant with mankind.

The Promise

Genesis 3:15 And I will put enmity between you and the woman, and between your seed and her Seed; He shall bruise your head, and you shall bruise His heel.

Speaking to Satan, God said the Seed of the woman would bruise his head and that Satan would bruise His heal.

From the moment Satan heard God was going to send a Redeemer for mankind through the Seed of the woman, his purpose was to destroy all the seed of the woman.

As generations passed, men and women ignored God and became more and more wicked. Satan's demons had even united with women to create a new being half-human, half-demon, in an attempt to corrupt the human race.

Genesis 6:4a There were giants on the earth in those days, and also afterward, when the sons of God came in to the daughters of men and they bore children to them.

This was Satan's attempt to stop *"the Seed of the woman"* (Christ) who was to come and crush his head.

This was the same spirit that entered into Pharaoh at the time of Moses' birth, and into King Herod at the time of Jesus' birth. This satanic spirit still desires to kill babies to stop the plan of God for mankind. It is continuing to induce the killing of babies through abortion.

NOAHIC COVENANT (Conditional)

The Blessings

After the flood, God made a covenant with Noah which confirmed His original covenants and gave a fuller revelation of His great love-plan of redemption for mankind. Just as God had given Adam and Eve authority over all that dwelt on the earth, He gave it to Noah.

Genesis 9:1,2 So God blessed Noah and his sons, and said to them: "Be fruitful and multiply, and fill the earth. And the fear of you and the dread of you shall be on every beast of the earth, on every bird of the air, on all that moves on the earth, and on all the fish of the sea. They are given into your hand."

Genesis 9:9,10a And as for Me, behold, I establish My covenant with you and with your descendants after you, and with every living creature that is with you ...

Two Conditions
➢ *Not to Eat Blood*

God instructed Noah that he and his family weren't to eat blood.

Genesis 9:4 But you shall not eat flesh with its life, that is, its blood.

➢ *Not to Kill Humans*

They weren't to kill another human.

Genesis 9:6 Whoever sheds man's blood, by man his blood shall be shed; for in the image of God He made man.

Satan's next attack on the human race would be in these two areas.

Jesus was to come as a human sacrifice for all mankind. His blood would be the propitiation for all mankind. How could Satan fight this?

By making human sacrifices common.

These same practices continue through Satan worshipers today.

A Visible Sign

This covenant had a visible sign. God promised He would never again destroy the whole earth with a flood and that the rainbow was a sign of this.

Genesis 9:12-15 And God said: "This is the sign of the covenant which I make between Me and you, and every living creature that is with you, for perpetual generations: I set My rainbow in the cloud, and it shall be for the sign of the covenant between Me and the earth. It shall be, when I bring a cloud over the earth, that the rainbow shall be seen in the cloud; and I will remember My covenant which is between Me and you and every living creature of all flesh; the waters shall never again become a flood to destroy all flesh."

ABRAHAMIC COVENANT (Conditional)

Even as mankind grew more and more wicked before the flood, they continued in wickedness after the flood. The children of Noah didn't walk upright before God, and neither did their descendants.

Then God spoke to Abraham, called him out, and renewed His covenant with mankind. Now God moved from dealing directly with all mankind, all of the descendants of Noah, to calling a particular family who was to represent Himself.

Note: In the following few verses, the conditions are underlined. The blessings are in brackets

Genesis 12:1-3 Now the LORD had said to Abram: "Get out of your country, from your kindred and from your father's house, to a land that I will show you. [I will make you a great nation; I will bless you and make your name great; and you shall be a blessing. I will bless those who bless you, and I will curse him who curses you; and in you all the families of the earth shall be blessed."]

With Isaac

God renewed this covenant with Isaac.

Genesis 26:3,4 Sojourn in this land, and [I will be with you and bless you; for to you and your descendants I give all these lands, and I will perform the oath which I swore to Abraham your father. And I will make your descendants multiply as the stars of heaven; I will give to your descendants all these lands; and in your seed all the nations of the shall be blessed.]

With Jacob

God renewed the covenant with Jacob.

Genesis 28:13,14 And behold, the LORD stood above it and said: "I am the LORD God of Abraham your father and the God of Isaac; [the land on which you lie I will give to you and your descendants. Also your descendants shall be as the dust of the earth; you shall spread abroad to the west and the east, to the north and the south; and in you and in your seed all the families of the earth shall be blessed.]

With Us

God renewed the covenant with us!

Galatians 3:14 [That the blessing of Abraham might come upon the Gentiles in Christ Jesus, that we might receive the promise of the Spirit] through faith.

Galatians 3:28,29 There is neither Jew nor Greek, there is neither slave nor free, there is neither male nor female; for you are all one in Christ Jesus. And if you are Christ's, [then you are Abraham's seed, and heirs according to the promise.]

By faith and obedience, we as God's covenant children can walk in all of the covenant blessings of Abraham, Isaac, and Jacob.

MOSAIC COVENANT (Conditional)

The seed of Abraham multiplied, and then, during a time of drought, God moved them to Egypt. First they were guests, then they were slaves. Finally after four hundred years, God called Moses to lead His people out of slavery and back into abundance.

Exodus 3:7,8a And the LORD said: "I have surely seen the oppression of My people who are in Egypt, and have heard their cry because of their taskmasters, for I know their sorrows. So I have come down to deliver them out of the hand of the Egyptians, and to bring them up from that land to a good and large land, to a land flowing with milk and honey."

We are going to skip over all that happened from this time until three months after the children of Israel were delivered from the land of Egypt.

The Covenant Given

Exodus 19:3-6b And Moses went up to God, and the LORD called to him from the mountain, saying, "Thus you shall say to the house of Jacob, and tell the children of Israel: `You have seen what I did to the Egyptians, and how I bore you on eagles' wings and brought you to Myself.

Now therefore, <u>if you will indeed obey My voice and keep My covenant,</u> [then you shall be a special treasure to Me above all people; for all the earth is Mine. And you shall be to Me a kingdom of priests and a holy nation.'"]

As covenant children of God, we too will be borne on "eagle's wings" out of bondage. If we obey His voice and keep His covenant, we too shall be a special treasure to God. As covenant children, we too are a kingdom of priests and a holy nation.

PALESTINIAN COVENANT (Conditional)

The children of Israel had been in the wilderness, and God had given them the Law. He followed this with the blessing if they kept the Law and the cursings if they didn't.

The blessings and the cursings of this covenant are given in Deuteronomy 28:1-68. These blessings and cursings were for Abraham and all of his descendants. They passed on to the nation of Israel, and then in the New Testament, we are told that we are the children of Abraham and these blessings can be ours.

The Blessings

How were the children of Israel to receive these blessings? By obeying the voice of the Lord.

Deuteronomy 28:1,2 Now it shall come to pass, if you diligently obey the voice of the LORD your God, to observe carefully all His commandments which I command you today, that the LORD your God will set you high above all nations of the earth. And all these blessings shall come upon you and overtake you, because you obey the voice of the LORD your God ...

If we obey the voice of the Lord, if we observe carefully His commandments, the blessings will naturally follow. They'll come upon us and overtake us!

Read Deuteronomy 28:3-14 substituting personal pronouns. For example:

"Blessed shall I be in the city, and blessed shall I be in the country. Blessed shall be the fruit of my body, the produce of my ground and the increase of my herds ..."

The Conditions

Why would the nation of Israel receive the cursings?

Because they didn't obey His voice. They didn't observe His commandments and statutes.

Deuteronomy 28:15 But it shall come to pass, if you do not obey the voice of the LORD your God, to observe carefully all His commandments and His statutes which I command you today, that all these curses will come upon you and overtake you ...

If we, as God's covenant children, will *"diligently obey"* the voice of the Lord and observe carefully all of His commandments, then we too will be blessed. God will open to us His good treasure, and bless the work of our hands.

DAVIDIC COVENANT (Unconditional)

God renewed the promise of the coming Seed He had made with Adam and Eve, and with Abraham.

2 Samuel 7:12,13 When your days are fulfilled and you rest with your fathers, I will set up your seed after you, who will come from your body, and I will establish his kingdom. He shall build a house for My name, and I will establish the throne of his kingdom forever.

The Promise

The Seed (the Messiah) would come through David, and He would establish a kingdom which would last forever.

As part of the Everlasting Covenant, we don't look forward for a promised Seed; we accept by faith, that Jesus is the promised One. As covenant children, we can see the kingdom of God established on this earth.

We can reign as kings as we take dominion over the earth, and everything in it. We can fulfill the Creator's purpose for our lives. We can walk in the blessing of our Everlasting Covenant with God. The conditions are still the same – faith and obedience.

QUESTIONS FOR REVIEW

1. Describe the difference between a conditional and an unconditional covenant.

2. List the covenants discussed in this lesson.

3. Why is it important for you to understand these covenants today?

Major Messianic Prophecies

Given	Subject	Fulfilled
Genesis 3:15	Seed of a woman	Galatians 4:4
Genesis 12:3	Descendant of Abraham	Matthew 1:1
Genesis 17:19	Descendant of Isaac	Luke 3:34
Numbers 24:17	Kingly descendant of Jacob	Matthew 1:2
Genesis 49:10	King from tribe of Judah	Luke 3:33
1 Samuel 2:10	Will be a King	Luke 19:38
Isaiah 9:7	Heir to throne of David	Luke 1:32,33
Psalms 45:6,7	Anointed and eternal	Hebrews 1:8-12
Micah 5:2	Born in Bethlehem	Luke 2:407
Isaiah 7:14	To be born of a virgin	Luke 1:26-31
Jeremiah 31:15	Massacre of infants	Matthew 2:16
Hosea 11:1	Flight to Egypt	Matthew 2:14,15
Malachi 3:1	Preceded by a forerunner	Luke 7:24,27
Psalms 2:7	Declared the Son of God	Matthew 3:17
Isaiah 9:1,2	Galilean ministry	Matthew 4:13-16
Isaiah 11:2	Some of His characteristics	Luke 2:52
Psalms 78:2-4	Speaks in parables	Matthew 13:34,35
Deuteronomy 18:15	Will be prophet like Moses	Acts 3:20,22
Isaiah 61:1,2	Will bind up brokenhearted	Luke 4:18,19
Isaiah 53:3	Rejected by His own people	John 1:11
Psalms 110:4	Priest after order of Melchizedek	Hebrews 5:5,6
Zechariah 9:9	Triumphal entry	Mark 11:7,9
Daniel 9:25	Time of Triumphal entry	Luke 2:1,2;3:23;19:42
Psalms 8:2	Adored by infants	Matthew 21:15,16
Isaiah 53:1	Not believed	John 12:37,38
Psalms 41:9	Betrayed by close friend	Luke 22:47,48
Zechariah 11:12	Betrayed for 30 pieces of silver	Matthew 26:14,15
Zechariah 11:13	Money returned/Potter's Field	Matthew 27:6,7
Psalms 109:7,8	Judas' office taken by another	Acts 1:18-20
Psalms 22:7,8	False witnesses accuse Him	Matthew 26:60,61
Psalms 35:11	Accused by false witnesses	Mark 14:57,58
Isaiah 53:7	Silent to accusations	Mark 15:4,5
Isaiah 50:6	Spat on and struck	Matthew 26:67
Psalms 35:19	Hated without reason	Matthew 26:67
Psalms 69:4	Hated without a cause	John 15:23-25
Isaiah 53:5	Vicarious sacrifice	Romans 5:6,8
Isaiah 53:12	Crucified with criminals	Mark 15:27,28
Zechariah 12:10	Pierced through hands and feet	John 20:27
Psalms 22:7,8	Sneered at and mocked	Luke 23:35
Psalms 69:9	Reproached	Romans 15:3
Psalms 109:4	Prayed for His enemies	Luke 23:34
Psalms 22:17,18	Gambled for His clothing	Matthew 27:35,36
Psalms 22:1	Forsaken by God	Matthew 27:46
Psalms 34:20	No bones broken	John 19:32-36
Psalms 69:21	Gave gall and vinegar to drink	Matthew 27:34
Zechariah 12:10	His side pierced	John 19:34
Isaiah 53:9	Buried with the rich	Matthew 27:57-60
Psalms 16:10	To be resurrected	Mark 16:6,7
Psalms 68:18	Ascension to God's right hand	Mark 16:19

Christ Revealed in the Old Testament

Some call the Old Testament the book of history. It is history – but even more it is *"His story."* From the creation of the world and of mankind, when God said, *Let us make man in our image*, to the fall of the nation of Israel, Christ is revealed in every book.

There are 330 prophecies concerning the coming Messiah in the Old Testament. They started general in nature, but as time passed, they became more specific.

The fulfillment of these marvelous prophecies in the person of Jesus Christ is irrefutable proof that Jesus is the Son of God – the One sent to redeem mankind from the penalties of sin.

Note: To save room in this lesson, we have not always given the New Testament verses of fullfilment. They are listed in the chart on the preceding page.

THE COMING MESSIAH

Seed of Woman

As mentioned before, the first prophecy of Jesus was that He was to be the Seed of the woman.

Genesis 3:15 And I will put enmity between you and the woman, and between your seed and her Seed; He shall bruise your head, and you shall bruise His heel.

Paul referred to the fulfillment of this prophecy.

Galatians 4:4, But when the fullness of the time had come, God sent forth His Son, born of a woman, born under the law ...

The coming Messiah was promised to Adam and Eve, Abraham, Isaac, Jacob, and David.

At first, it seemed the promised Seed could be from any woman. Then the prophecies became more specific. The promise would be fulfilled in Abraham's descendants, from Isaac – from Jacob – from David. The prophecies of His lineage became more and more specific.

Born in Bethlehem

It was prophesied that the Messiah would be born in Bethlehem, and Jesus was.

Micah 5:2 But you, Bethlehem Ephrathah, though you are little among the thousands of Judah, yet out of you shall come forth to Me the One to be ruler in Israel, whose goings forth have been from of old, from everlasting.

Luke 2:4-7 And Joseph also went up from Galilee, out of the city of Nazareth, into Judea, to the city of David, which is called Bethlehem, because he was of the house and lineage of David, to be registered with Mary, his betrothed wife, who was with child. So it was, that while they were there, the days were completed for her to be delivered. And she brought forth her firstborn Son, and wrapped Him in swaddling cloths, and laid Him in a manger, because there was no room for them in the inn.

Prophet like Moses

The Messiah would be a prophet like Moses.

Deuteronomy 18:15a The LORD your God will raise up for you a Prophet like me from your midst, from your brethren.

Priest like Melchizedek

He would be a priest after the order of Melchizedek.

Psalms 110:4 The LORD has sworn and will not relent, "You are a priest forever according to the order of Melchizedek."

King like David

He would be heir to the throne of David.

Isaiah 9:7 Of the increase of His government and peace there will be no end, upon the throne of David and over His kingdom, to order it and establish it with judgment and justice from that time forward, even forever. The zeal of the LORD of hosts will perform this.

Luke 1:32,33 He will be great, and will be called the Son of the Highest; and the Lord God will give Him the throne of His father David. And He will reign over the house of Jacob forever, and of His kingdom there will be no end.

Time of Coming

The Messiah would come at a particular time in history. He would offer Himself as the King of Israel, and be rejected.

Daniel 9:25,26b Know therefore and understand, that from the going forth of the command to restore and build Jerusalem until Messiah the Prince, there shall be seven weeks and sixty-two weeks; the street shall be built again, and the wall, even in troublesome times. And after the sixty-two weeks Messiah shall be cut off, but not for Himself ...

THE PROPHESIES OF DAVID

It seems David entered into, and understood more about, the suffering of Christ than any of the other prophets. Through his own suffering, he gives us insights into the very feelings of Christ as He hung on the cross – even when He was in the depths of the earth. He describes Jesus coming back into the throne room of heaven in exaltation.

Prophecies of the Betrayal
➤ *Betrayed by Friend*

David prophesied that Jesus would be betrayed by a friend, that the days of this friend would be few, and that he would be replaced by another.

Psalms 41:9 Even my own familiar friend in whom I trusted, who ate my bread, has lifted up his heel against me.

Psalms 109:8 Let his days be few, and let another take his office.

➤ *False Witnesses Accuse Him*

David prophesied they would bring false witness against Him.

Psalms 27:12 Do not deliver me to the will of my adversaries; for false witnesses have risen against me, and such as breathe out violence.

Matthew confirms this prophecy.

Matthew 26:60b,61 But at last two false witnesses came forward and said, "This fellow said, `I am able to destroy the temple of God and to build it in three days.' "

➤ *Hated without cause*

He would be hated without a cause.

Psalms 69:4 Those who hate me without a cause are more than the hairs of my head; they are mighty who would destroy me, being my enemies wrongfully; though I have stolen nothing, I still must restore it.

John confirmed this prophecy and even quoted from it.

John 15:23-25 He who hates Me hates My Father also. If I had not done among them the works which no one else did, they would have no sin; but now they have seen and also hated both Me and My Father. But this happened that the word might be fulfilled which is written in their law, `They hated Me without a cause.'

Prophesies of Crucifixion

There are many prophecies of the crucificion. The fullfilment is found in Matthew 27, Mark 15, Luke 23, John 19.

➤ *Hands and Feet Pierced*
➤ *Soldiers Cast Lots for Coat*

Psalms 22:16-19 For dogs have surrounded Me; the assembly of the wicked has enclosed Me. They pierced My hands and My feet; I can count all My bones. They look and stare at Me. They divide My garments among them, and for My clothing they cast lots. But You, O LORD, do not be far from Me; O My Strength, hasten to help Me!

➤ *Reproached, Despised,
Laughed At*

➤ *Prophetic Words Repeated in
Mockery*

Psalms 22:6-8 But I am a worm, and no man; a reproach of men, and despised of the people. All those who see Me laugh Me to scorn; they shoot out the lip, they shake the head, saying, "He trusted in the LORD, let Him rescue Him; let Him deliver Him, since He delights in Him!"

➤ *Given Gall and Vinegar*

Psalms 69:21 They also gave me gall for my food, and for my thirst they gave me vinegar to drink.

➤ *Prayed for Enemies*

Psalms 109:4,5 In return for my love they are my accusers, but I give myself to prayer. Thus they have rewarded me evil for good, and hatred for my love.

➤ *Not a Bone Broken*

Psalms 34:20 He guards all his bones; not one of them is broken.

His Resurrection / Ascension

The fulfillment of these prophecies are found in Matthew 28, Mark 16, Luke 24, and John 20.

➤ *Even in Death*

Jesus knew even as He was dying that God wouldn't leave His soul in the depths of the earth. David gives us His thoughts at this time.

Psalms 16:10 For You will not leave my soul in Sheol, nor will You allow Your Holy One to see corruption.

➤ *The Triumph*

David has even given us a wonderful description of Jesus coming back into the throne room of heaven.

Psalms 24:7-10 Lift up your heads, O you gates! And be lifted up, you everlasting doors! And the King of glory shall come in. Who is this King of glory? The LORD strong and mighty, The LORD mighty in battle. Lift up your heads, O you gates! And lift them up, you everlasting doors! And the King of glory shall come in. Who is this King of glory? The LORD of hosts, He is the King of glory. Selah

Psalms 68:18 You have ascended on high, You have led captivity captive; You have received gifts among men, even among the rebellious, that the LORD God might dwell there.

THE PROPHESIES OF ISAIAH

The details of Isaiah's prophecies are awesome. Isaiah fifty-three gives the most complete description of Jesus' death. It was so detailed that the early Jewish religious leaders claimed it hadn't been part of their Scripture – that it had been added by Jewish Christians.

In 1947, the Dead Sea Scrolls were discovered. These are the most ancient scrolls of the Bible ever found. Only one scroll survived with no break from the beginning to the end. It was the writings of Isaiah, and it contained the fifty-third chapter.

Read Isaiah fifty-three before going on to the specifics of Isaiah's prophecies.

Jesus identified with the prophecies of Isaiah when He quoted Isaiah 61:1,2.

Luke 4:18,19 The Spirit of the LORD is upon Me, because He has anointed Me to preach the gospel to the poor. He has sent Me to heal the brokenhearted, to preach deliverance to the captives and recovery of sight to the blind, to set at liberty those who are oppressed, to preach the acceptable year of the LORD.

Jesus' History

Some of the Old Testament prophecies of Jesus deal with His unique birth, family line, and anointing.

➤ *Virgin Birth*

Isaiah 7:14 Therefore the LORD Himself will give you a sign: behold, the virgin shall conceive and bear a Son, and shall call His name Immanuel.

➤ *Family*

Isaiah 11:1 There shall come forth a Rod from the stem of Jesse, and a Branch shall grow out of his roots.

➤ *Anointing*

Isaiah 11:2a The Spirit of the LORD shall rest upon Him ...

Jesus' Characteristics
➤ *Wisdom*

Isaiah 11:2 The Spirit of the LORD shall rest upon Him, the Spirit of wisdom and understanding, the Spirit of counsel and might, the Spirit of knowledge and of the fear of the LORD.

➤ *Spiritual Discerning*

Isaiah 11:3 His delight is in the fear of the LORD, and He shall not judge by the sight of His eyes, nor decide by the hearing of His ears ...

➤ *Justice*

Isaiah 11:4 But with righteousness He shall judge the poor, and decide with equity for the meek of the earth; He shall strike the earth with the rod of His mouth, and with the breath of His lips He shall slay the wicked.

➤ *Righteousness*

Isaiah 11:5 Righteousness shall be the belt of His loins, and faithfulness the belt of His waist.

➤ *Silence*

Isaiah 42:2 He will not cry out, nor raise His voice, nor cause His voice to be heard in the street.

Isaiah 53:7 He was oppressed and He was afflicted, yet He opened not His mouth; He was led as a lamb to the slaughter, and as a sheep before its shearers is silent, so He opened not his mouth.

➤ *Gentleness*

Isaiah 42:3 A bruised reed He will not break, and smoking flax He will not quench; He will bring forth justice for truth.

➤ *Perseverance*

Isaiah 42:4 He will not fail nor be discouraged, till He has established justice in the earth; and the coastlands shall wait for His law.

➤ *Radiance*

Isaiah 42:6 I, the LORD, have called You in righteousness, and will hold Your hand; I will keep You and give You as a covenant to the people, as a light to the Gentiles.

Isaiah 9:2 The people who walked in darkness have seen a great light; those who dwelt in the land of the shadow of death, upon them a light has shined.

➤ *Compassion*

Isaiah 53:4 Surely He has borne our griefs and carried our sorrows; yet we esteemed Him stricken, smitten by God, and afflicted.

➤ *Meekness*

Isaiah 53:7 He was oppressed and He was afflicted, yet He opened not His mouth; He was led as a lamb to the slaughter, and as a sheep before its shearers is silent, so He opened not his mouth.

➤ *Vicarious Sufferings*

Isaiah 53:10 Yet it pleased the LORD to bruise Him; He has put Him to grief. When You make His soul an offering for sin, He shall see His seed, He shall prolong His days, and the pleasure of the LORD shall prosper in His hand.

➤ *Sinlessness*

Isaiah 53:9 And they made His grave with the wicked-but with the rich at His death, because He had done no violence, nor was any deceit in His mouth.

➤ *Greatness*

Isaiah 53:12 Therefore I will divide Him a portion with the great, and He shall divide the spoil with the strong, because He poured out His soul unto death, and He was numbered with the transgressors, and He bore the sin of many, and made intercession for the transgressors.

➤ *Saving Power*

Isaiah 53:11 He shall see the travail of His soul, and be satisfied: by His knowledge My righteous Servant shall justify many, for He shall bear their iniquities.

Jesus' Mission

➤ *Illuminator*

Isaiah 9:2 The people who walked in darkness have seen a great light; those who dwelt in the land of the shadow of death, upon them a light has shined.

➤ *Judge*

Isaiah 11:3 His delight is in the fear of the LORD, and He shall not judge by the sight of His eyes, nor decide by the hearing of His ears.

➤ *Reprover*

Isaiah 11:4 But with righteousness He shall judge the poor, and decide with equity for the meek of the earth; He shall strike the earth with the rod of His mouth, and with the breath of His lips He shall slay the wicked.

➤ *Law-giver*

Isaiah 42:4 He will not fail nor be discouraged, till He has established justice in the earth; and the coastlands shall wait for His law.

➤ *Liberator*

Isaiah 42:7 To open blind eyes, to bring out prisoners from the prison, those who sit in darkness from the prison house.

➤ *Burden-bearer*

Isaiah 53:4 Surely He has borne our griefs and carried our sorrows; yet we esteemed Him stricken, smitten by God, and afflicted.

➤ *Sin-bearer*

Isaiah 53:6 All we like sheep have gone astray; we have turned, every one, to his own way; and the LORD has laid on Him the iniquity of us all.

➤ *Intercessor*

Isaiah 53:12 Therefore I will divide Him a portion with the great, and He shall divide the spoil with the strong, because He poured out His soul unto death, and He was numbered with the transgressors, and He bore the sin of many, and made intercession for the transgressors.

➤ *Only Savior*

Isaiah 53:5 But He was wounded for our transgressions, He was bruised for our iniquities; the chastisement for our peace was upon Him, and by His stripes we are healed.

➤ *Healer*

Isaiah 53:5b ... and by His stripes we are healed.

Jesus' Titles
➢ *Immanuel*

Isaiah 7:14 Therefore the LORD Himself will give you a sign: Behold, the virgin shall conceive and bear a Son, and shall call His name Immanuel.

➢ *Wonderful, Counselor, Mighty God, Everlasting Father, Prince of Peace*

Isaiah 9:6 For unto us a Child is born, unto us a Son is given; and the government will be upon His shoulder. And His name will be called Wonderful, Counselor, Mighty God, Everlasting Father, Prince of Peace.

➢ *Righteous King*

Isaiah 32:1 Behold, a king will reign in righteousness, and princes will rule with justice.

➢ *My Elect One*

Isaiah 42:1 Behold! My Servant whom I uphold, My Elect One in whom My soul delights! I have put My Spirit upon Him; He will bring forth justice to the Gentiles.

➢ *Arm of the Lord*

Isaiah 53:1 Who has believed our report? and to whom has the arm of the LORD been revealed?

➢ *Anointed Preacher*

Isaiah 61:1 The Spirit of the LORD God is upon Me, because the LORD has anointed Me to preach good tidings to the poor; He has sent Me to heal the brokenhearted, to proclaim liberty to the captives, and the opening of the prison to those who are bound.

Summary

The 330 prophecies of the Old Testament, telling of the coming Messiah, were all fulfilled in Christ. It is impossible for this many prophecies to "just happen" to be fulfilled in one man. It cannot be coincidental. Jesus is the Son of God. He is the One portrayed throughout all the Old Testament. He is the Savior of mankind.

QUESTIONS FOR REVIEW

1. What was the first prophecy recorded in the Scripture regarding the coming Messiah? How did it become more specific?

2. List three prophecies found in Scripture that reveal that the coming Messiah would function as Prophet, Priest, and King.

3. List two major prophecies from both the book of Psalms and the book of Isaiah which reveal a major aspect of the coming redemptive work of Jesus Christ.

The Tabernacle of Moses

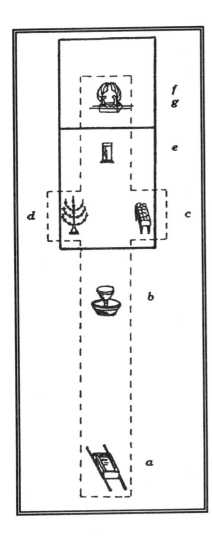

The Holy of Holies – God the Father

Open to High Priest Once a Year

Furniture:

f **Ark of the Covenant** – Presence of God

g **The Mercy Seat** – The Throne of God

The Holy Place – God the Son

Open to Priests Only

Furniture:

c **Table of Shewbread** – Jesus, the Bread of Life

d **Golden Lampstand** – Jesus, the Light of the World

e **Altar of Incense** – Jesus, the Intercessor

The Court – God the Holy Spirit

Open to All Believers

Furniture:

a **Altar of Sacrifice** – Jesus, the Supreme Sacrifice

b **The Laver** – Jesus, the Word of God that Cleanses

Symbol of the Church – Habitation of God Through the Spirit

> **Ephesians 2:19-22** *Now, therefore, you are no longer strangers and foreigners, but fellow citizens with the saints and members of the household of God, having been built on the foundation of the apostles and prophets, Jesus Christ Himself being the chief cornerstone, in whom the whole building, being joined together, grows into a holy temple in the Lord, in whom you also are being built together for a habitation of God in the Spirit.*

Symbol of the Believer – The Temple of God

> **2 Corinthians 6:16b** *For you are the temple of the living God. As God has said: "I will dwell in them and walk among them. I will be their God, and they shall be My people."*

Type of Things in the Heavens

> **Hebrews 8:5** *who serve the copy and shadow of the heavenly things, as Moses was divinely instructed when he was about to make the tabernacle. For He said, "See that you make all things according to the pattern shown you on the mountain."*

> **Hebrews 9:23** *Therefore it was necessary that the copies of the things in the heavens should be purified with these, but the heavenly things themselves with better sacrifices than these.*

Lesson Five

Patterns for Worship and Service

Types, Patterns and Shadows

Type:
Prefiguring what is to come (prototype)
Symbol:
Represents something else not tied to time
You can have symbols within types, but not types within symbols
Example:
Feast of Passover – type of deliverance of sinners by Christ's sacrifice
Lamb of Passover – symbolic of Christ

All through the Old Testament, God gave types, patterns, and shadows of the coming Redeemer.

God gave the Law to Moses soon after the children of Israel left Egypt. They could not become a nation until they had a unifying set of laws under which they operated. The Law had two parts – one for the protection of the people through civil and dietary laws – the other to provide redemption through the person of Jesus Christ. The Law pointed forward to Christ.

God also gave Moses exact instructions for making the tabernacle. Every part of the tabernacle was a symbol. Every part spoke of the life and death of the coming Messiah. In this lesson, we will study the tabernacle and the offerings.

Jesus said He didn't come to destroy the Law, but to fulfill it.

Matthew 5:17 Do not think that I came to destroy the Law or the Prophets. I did not come to destroy but to fulfill.

It is necessary to know about the tabernacle, offerings, feasts, and the priests, to understand such verses as the following.

Hebrews 8:1-3b,5 Now this is the main point of the things we are saying: We have such a High Priest, who is seated at the right hand of the throne of the Majesty in the heavens, a Minister of the sanctuary and of the true tabernacle which the LORD erected, and not man. For every high priest is appointed to offer both gifts and sacrifices.

Who serve the copy and shadow of the heavenly things, as Moses was divinely instructed when he was about to make the tabernacle. For He said, "See that you make all things according to the pattern shown you on the mountain."

THE TABERNACLE

The pattern for the tabernacle was given to Moses – the measurements, wood, material, gold and silver, jewels, linen, and wool. They all had definite meanings – they all pointed forward to Christ.

Three Divisions

There were three sections of the tabernacle which were symbolic of the three distinct personalities of God – the Father, Son, and Holy Spirit. They were also symbolic of the body, soul, and spirit of mankind.

➤ *The Courtyard*

The first area was the courtyard. All the people could go into the courtyard – both the Jews and the Gentile converts to Judaism. The courtyard represents the Holy Spirit who works with all mankind to bring them to Christ.

➤ *The Holy Place*

The priests could go into the Holy Place. They made sacrifices in the courtyard, and also in the Holy Place. The Holy Place represents Jesus who is our Sacrifice.

➤ *The Holy of Holies*

Only the high priest could go into the Holy of Holies on the Day of Atonement. He spent time sanctifying himself before entering the Holy of Holies to make sacrifices for the people. If there was sin in his life, he would die. The Holy of Holies represents the presence of God.

The Holy of Holies was separated from the Holy Place by a very thick, woven curtain or veil. When Jesus died on the cross, this veil was supernaturally torn from the top to the bottom, signifying there was no longer a need for a separate Holy of Holies.

There is no longer a need for a priest to come into God's presence for us! Jesus became our High Priest and we can come directly to Him. We can come boldly into the presence of God.

Matthew 27:50,51 Jesus, when He had cried out again with a loud voice, yielded up His spirit. And behold, the veil of the temple was torn in two from top to bottom; and the earth quaked, and the rocks were split ...

When Jesus became the sacrifice for the whole world, there was no longer a need for a temple or tabernacle. Their purpose was fulfilled in Him. The furniture, feasts, offerings, and priests were all pictures of Jesus and what He would do for mankind.

Today, when we are entering into praise and then worship, it is good to remember the three divisions of the tabernacle. They represent how we come into the presence of God. First, we enter the gates with thanksgiving. Second, we enter His courts with praise for what He has done for us. Finally, we proceed into the Holy of Holies, and spend time worshiping the Lord for who He is.

THE FURNITURE

Every piece of furniture in the tabernacle represented Jesus. It was designed as a physical representation of the Redeemer of all mankind. The material out of which each item was fashioned had a special significance.

➤ Gold – the manifestation of Deity
➤ Silver – redemption
➤ Brass – judgment

The colors of the various coverings also had special significance.

➢ Blue – heavenly in nature or origin
➢ Purple – royalty
➢ Scarlet – sacrifice

Acacia wood was an almost indestructible wood and it represented *"an incorruptible Christ."*

In the Courtyard
➢ *Brazen Altar*

Everyone could come into the courtyard. As they came through the gate, the first thing they saw was the brazen altar. This was also called the altar of burnt offering. It was here, as they first came to God, sacrifices were made for their sins. The altar was made of acacia wood and of bronze. The acacia wood represented the incorruptible Christ and the bronze represented judgment for sins.

The sacrifices made on this altar represented the final sacrifice that would be made by the Son of God.

Hebrews 9:26b ... but now, once at the end of the ages, He has appeared to put away sin by the sacrifice of Himself.

Jesus became our sacrifice for the forgiveness of our sins. Now we are to present our bodies a living sacrifice to Him.

Romans 12:1 I beseech you therefore, brethren, by the mercies of God, that you present your bodies a living sacrifice, holy, acceptable to God, which is your reasonable service.

➢ *The Laver*

The laver made from bronze was the next piece of furniture. It was filled with water and the priests were to wash their hands and feet before ministering. This washing was done as often as needed and signified Christ cleansing us from every spot, wrinkle, and blemish.

Ephesians 5:25b,-27 ... just as Christ also loved the church and gave Himself for it, that He might sanctify and cleanse it with the washing of water by the word, that He might present it to Himself a glorious church, not having spot or wrinkle or any such thing, but that it should be holy and without blemish.

After we receive salvation, there is a need for continuous cleansing. If we sin, we are to confess our sins and receive forgiveness.

1 John 1:9 If we confess our sins, He is faithful and just to forgive us our sins and to cleanse us from all unrighteousness.

There is also to be a continuous feeding upon the Word of God.

John 15:3 You are already clean because of the word which I have spoken to you.

In the Holy Place

There were three pieces of furniture in the Holy Place. The table of showbread on the right side, the golden candlestick on the left, and the altar of incense directly in front.

➢ *Table of Showbread*

The table of showbread was made of acacia wood and covered with gold. It represented the humanity and deity of Christ. Bread was always kept on this table and it signifies Christ – the Bread of Life.

1 Corinthians 10:16,17 The cup of blessing which we bless, is it not the communion of the blood of Christ? The bread which we break, is it not the communion of the body of Christ? For we, being many, are one bread and one body; for we all partake of that one bread.

Paul wrote that we are one body – bread. Jesus is the bread, and in Him we are also the bread.

➢ *Golden Candlestick*

The candlestick was made of pure gold, and it represented Christ as the true light.

The apostle John wrote,

John 8:12 Then Jesus spoke to them again, saying, "I am the light of the world. He who follows Me shall not walk in darkness, but have the light of life."

As we follow Jesus, we walk in His light and become light for others.

Matthew 5:16 Let your light so shine before men, that they may see your good works and glorify your Father in heaven.

➢ *Altar of Incense*

The altar of incense was also made of acacia wood covered with gold. The continuous burning of incense signified Christ as our intercessor.

Romans 8:34 Who is he who condemns? It is Christ who died, and furthermore is also risen, who is even at the right hand of God, who also makes intercession for us.

We are to continue the sacrifice of incense on a daily basis through prayer.

Revelation 8:3,4 Then another angel, having a golden censer, came and stood at the altar. And he was given much incense, that he should offer it with the prayers of all the saints upon the golden altar which was before the throne. And the smoke of the incense, with the prayers of the saints, ascended before God from the angel's hand.

In the Holy of Holies
➢ *Ark of the Covenant*

In the Holy of Holies there were two pieces of furniture – the ark of the covenant and the mercy seat. Aaron's rod, the tablets of stone, and manna were in the ark.

The ark was formed from acacia wood and gold, and again these materials signified the humanity and deity of Christ.

It was at the ark that Moses could find the presence of God. Today Jesus is our meeting place with God.

Exodus 25:22 And there I will meet with you, and I will speak with you from above the mercy seat, from between the two cherubim which are on the ark of the Testimony, of all things which I will give you in commandment to the children of Israel.

➢ *Mercy Seat*

The mercy seat was formed of pure gold representing pure Deity. On top of the ark, at the ends of the mercy seat, there were two cherubim also formed of pure gold. The mercy seat typified the throne of God protected by His angelic creations.

Hebrews 4:16 Let us therefore come boldly to the throne of grace, that we may obtain mercy and find grace to help in time of need.

OFFERINGS

The offerings are as rich in meaning as the furniture and the feasts. All offerings and sacrifices had to be made in faith to be effective.

There were five main offerings, and they can be studied in detail in the first five chapters of Leviticus. They all represented different aspects of the one complete sacrifice – Jesus.

They can be divided into two divisions:
➢ Sweet Savor – typifying the perfect Christ who delights to do God's will
➢ Non-Sweet Savor – typifying Christ who bears the sinner's iniquities

Offerings of Sweet Savor
➢ *Burnt Offering*

The purpose of the burnt offering was to gain access to God.

It was to be either a bullock, a lamb, a goat, a turtledove, or a pigeon. Which animal or bird was decided by a man's possessions. It was to be the most a man could afford, and totally without spot and blemish.

It was a voluntary offering and a symbol of Christ offering Himself voluntarily, without spot, to God.

The person bringing the offering was to lay his hands on its head transferring his sins to the animal, and then slay it. This wasn't easy to do since this offering was to be known by the person bringing it and had often become a pet.

Neither was it easy for God to give His Son to die for our sins.

➢ *Meal Offering*

The purpose of the meal offering was to show thankfulness to God. It was made up of fine meal, oil, salt, and frankincense, and was also a voluntary offering.

The fine meal was to be perfect – no lumps, no coarseness, and no foreign material. It spoke of the perfection of Christ.

The oil spoke of the presence of the Holy Spirit in the life of Christ.

When frankincense is burned, it gives a wonderful fragrance. It spoke of the suffering of Jesus on our behalf and the perfection with which He would come through that time.

The salt spoke of the preservation of the offering.

In this offering, there was to be no leaven, which represents sin and false doctrine. There was to be no honey, which represents that which is very satisfying to the natural man. A handful of this offering was burned as an offering to God, and the remainder was for the use of the priests.

➢ *Peace Offering*

The purpose of the peace offering was to call for fellowship, intimacy with God, and celebration.

This offering was different in that a portion went to the Lord , a portion went to the priests and the rest went to the family making the sacrifice. It portrays Christ reconciling us to God.

The peace offering couldn't be made if there was sin in the life of the person that hadn't been made right. God cannot fellowship with sin.

Offerings of Non-Sweet Savor

➢ *Sin Offering*

The purpose of the sin offering was to cover the guilt of sin.

It was an offering of a bullock (if for a priest or the whole congregation), a young male goat (if a ruler), or a young female goat (if one wasn't a priest or a leader). In each case, the animal had to be without spot or blemish.

It is interesting to note that in the burnt offering, the offering was according to a person's ability to give. However, what was to be offered in the sin offering, had to do with a person's position. The offering for the sin of the priest was the greatest – greater than that of the ruler.

The person bringing the sacrifice, the person seeking forgiveness for his sins, was to bring the sacrifice to the temple in front of the people. He was to confess his sins. Then he was to slay the innocent animal that carried his sins. This pictures our need for repentance and our acceptance of our responsibility for the death of Christ for our sins.

Jesus, who knew no sin, became sin for us.

2 Corinthians 5:21 For He made Him who knew no sin to be sin for us, that we might become the righteousness of God in Him.

After the priest took the blood of the sacrifice and applied it to the altar of incense, he burned part of the sacrifice on the brazen altar, and then he took the rest of the sacrifice and burned it outside the camp.

In Hebrews, we read that Jesus suffered outside the gate.

Hebrews 13:12 Therefore Jesus also, that He might sanctify the people with His own blood, suffered outside the gate.

We are also to be willing to bear His reproach, to seek only Him, and to give praise continuously.

Hebrews 13:13-15 Therefore let us go forth to Him, outside the camp, bearing His reproach. For here we have no continuing city, but we seek the one to come. Therefore by Him let us continually offer the sacrifice of praise to God, that is, the fruit of our lips, giving thanks to His name.

➤ *Trespass Offering*

In the trespass offering, we have a picture of Christ making provision in His death for the injury of our sins.

Wouldn't it be wonderful if once we have accepted Jesus, there was never again a need to be cleansed from sin?

John wrote,

1 John 1:8-10 If we say that we have no sin, we deceive ourselves, and the truth is not in us. If we confess our sins, He is faithful and just to forgive us our sins and to cleanse us from all unrighteousness. If we say that we have not sinned, we make Him a liar, and His word is not in us.

The trespass offering was to deal with several areas in which a person was involved in the everyday affairs of life. It is important to study these six areas of trespass because these are areas many Christians are involved in today not realizing they are sin. How good it is to know, as we realize we have been in this type of sin, that we have instant forgiveness.

The first step to forgiveness was confession.

Leviticus 5:5 And it shall be, when he is guilty in any of these matters, that he shall confess that he has sinned in that thing.

The first step to being forgiven is still confession.

1 John 1:9 If we confess our sins, He is faithful and just to forgive us our sins and to cleanse us from all unrighteousness.

> *Six Kinds of Trespasses*

➡ **Sin of Swearing**

This had to do with telling the truth as in a court of law today. If a person knew the truth and didn't share it, it was sin.

Leviticus 5:1 If a person sins in hearing the utterance of an oath, and is a witness, whether he has seen or known of the matter--if he does not tell it, he bears guilt.

➡ **Sin of Defilement**

This sin had to do with touching the dead or the unclean even if it was hidden from him.

Leviticus 5:2 Or if a person touches any unclean thing, whether it is the carcass of an unclean beast, or the carcass of unclean livestock, or the carcass of unclean creeping things, and it is hidden from him, he also shall be unclean and guilty. Or if he touches human uncleanness, whatever sort of uncleanness it is with which a man may be defiled, and it is hidden from him-- when he realizes it, then he shall be guilty.

When it becomes known, it is sin. There is much defilement from the world around us today. There are things we may see without wishing to, or things we may have done without realizing they are evil.

➡ **Sin of Broken Promises**

God deals very firmly with broken promises. If we don't keep our word, we are unable to believe God to keep His.

We can only trust His Word to the point we know others can trust ours. We must learn to be people of our word. We must do what we say we will do.

Leviticus 5:4 Or if a person swears, speaking thoughtlessly with his lips to do evil or to do good, whatever it is that a man may pronounce by an oath, and it is hidden from him--when he realizes it, then he shall be guilty in any of these matters.

Numbers 30:2 If a man vows a vow to the LORD, or swears an oath to bind himself by some agreement, he shall not break his word; he shall do according to all that proceeds out of his mouth.

➡ **Sin About Holy Things**

Leviticus 5:15a If a person commits a trespass, and sins unintentionally in regard to the holy things of the LORD ...

The holy things of the Lord were all the items of the tabernacle, the feasts, and the offerings. These things were never to be taken lightly in action or in word. Today this could apply to:

> Being dishonest about things of the Lord – "the Lord told me to tell you," or "I spend thirty minutes a day in prayer" when you don't

> Wasting God-given talents

> Withholding tithes and offerings

➡ **Sins of Ignorance**

Leviticus 5:17 If a person sins, and commits any of these things which are forbidden to be done by the commandments of the LORD, though he does not know it, yet he is guilty and shall bear his iniquity.

➡ **Trespass Against the Lord**

It is interesting to note that the following list of things which are trespasses against the Lord are all sins against other people. For forgiveness to be given, it was, and is still necessary to restore these things to their rightful owner.

Leviticus 6:2-3 If a person sins and commits a trespass against the LORD ...

- **by lying to his neighbor about what was delivered to him for safekeeping,**
- **or about a pledge,**
- **or about a robbery,**
- **or if he has extorted from his neighbor,**
- **or if he has found what was lost and lies concerning it, and swears falsely**
- **in any one of these things that a man may do in which he sins: then it shall be, because he has sinned and is guilty, that he shall restore what he has stolen, or the thing which he has deceitfully obtained, or what was delivered to him for safekeeping, or the lost thing which he found ...**

Summary

As we have studied the layout of the tabernacle, the furniture and the offerings made there, we have learned they all pointed to the coming Redeemer. Jesus fulfilled every type, symbol, and shadow. He fulfilled every offering.

When we believe in Jesus Christ, we receive the sacrifice He made on our behalf. Through faith in Him we are set free from sin. We can rejoice as Jeremiah did in the book of Lamentations:

Lamentations 3:22,23 Through the LORD'S mercies we are not consumed, because His compassions fail not. They are new every morning; great is Your faithfulness.

QUESTIONS FOR REVIEW

1. What was symbolized by the three sections of the tabernacle?

2. What was symbolized by the three articles of furniture in the Holy Place.

3. List three offerings of sweet savor and two offerings of non-sweet savor.

Parallels Between Passover and Jesus' Sacrifice

Old Testament Reference	*New Testament Reference*
1. Period of examination for blemish – 3 1/2 days	
Exodus 12:3,5,6	John 18:38 (3 1/2 years)
2. The tested Lamb must be killed	
Exodus 12:6	John 12:24; Matthew 16:21
3. Shed Blood averts God's judgment	
Exodus 12:7,12,13	Hebrews 9:22, 12 John 1:7
4. Man must take some action to be saved	
Exodus 12:22	John 3:16
5. God's people must eat the flesh of the sacrifice as a remembrance	
Exodus 12:8-10	Mark 14:22
6. Jesus, as a lamb, did not plead for His life	
Isaiah 53:7	Matthew 27:13,14
7. Jesus died during the passover celebration	
	Mark 14:12; Mark 15:6
8. No bone of the lamb was to be broken	
Exodus 12:46, Numbers 9:12	John 19:33,36
9. Unbelievers may not partake of the flesh of the sacrifice	
Exodus 12:43,45,48	1 Corinthians 10:21
10. Christ called our Passover	
	1 Corinthians 5:7
11. Jesus died in the same city where the people were to celebrate the Passover	
Deuteronomy 16:2; 2 Kings 23:27	Mark 10:33

Compiled by Dr. Jack Tuls

Lesson Six

Feasts, Kings and Priests

FEASTS

The feasts of Israel were a time of rejoicing, a time of celebration, a time of giving thanks. They were in memorial of the great events in the history of the nation of Israel, but they were also a prophetic picture of events in the future. There were seven feasts.

➤ Feast of Passover
➤ Feast of Unleavened Bread
➤ Feast of Firstfruits
➤ Feast of Pentecost
➤ Feast of Trumpets
➤ Feast Day of Atonement
➤ Feast of Tabernacles

Passover (Pesach)

References: Exodus 12:1-14, 21-29; Leviticus 23:4,5; Numbers 33:3; Deuteronomy 16:1-8

The Passover Feast began on the night in Egypt when the children of Israel were instructed to sacrifice the lamb and put the blood on the doorpost with hyssop. It was fulfilled the day Jesus, the Lamb of God, was crucified for the sins of all mankind. Jesus was the Passover lamb slain before the foundation of the world.

Moses demanded that Pharaoh let God's people go. Pharaoh resisted, and plague after plague fell on the land of Egypt. The death of the first-born was the final plague.

God instructed Moses, who instructed the people, to prepare a sacrificial lamb. The blood of this lamb was to be sprinkled on both sides of the door and the top using hyssop. The placement of the blood was a picture of the cross. The blood wasn't applied with the stroking motion of a brush, but rather with a striking motion. This represented the shedding of Jesus' blood through the beatings He received.

The lamb was cooked with bitter herbs and eaten with unleavened bread. The bitter herbs represented the bitter suffering and death of Jesus, and the unleavened bread spoke of the sinlessness of Jesus. The sacrifice was eaten as the family stood, prepared for flight.

The children of Israel were free to make this sacrifice or not. Those who believed and applied the blood to their doorposts were spared the death of their first born.

Still, we are given a choice. We can believe God's word and accept the sacrifice Christ made for us, or we can refuse.

> **Taking communion has replaced the Passover.**
>
> *Eating of the flesh represents eating the body of Christ*
> *Jesus is the Word, and today we eat of His flesh by eating the Word of God.*
>
> **John wrote:**
>
> *In the beginning was the Word, and the Word was with God, and the Word was God ... and the Word became flesh and dwelt among us (John 1:1,14a)*

John 3:16-18 For God so loved the world that He gave His only begotten Son, that whoever believes in Him should not perish but have everlasting life. For God did not send His Son into the world to condemn the world, but that the world through Him might be saved. He who believes in Him is not condemned; but he who does not believe is condemned already, because he has not believed in the name of the only begotten Son of God.

The celebration of the Passover Feast was a reminder of God bringing the nation of Israel out of Egypt. It represented salvation from the slavery of Egypt. For us, it means salvation from the horrors of sin.

Christ was represented so many ways in this one feast that we have included a chart to show the parallels at the beginning of this lesson.

Unleavened Bread (Hag Ha Matzoh)

Reference: Exodus 12:8,15-20,31-39; 13:3-10; Leviticus 23:6-8; Numbers 28:17-25; Deuteronomy 16:1-8

Before the feasts of Passover, Unleavened Bread and Firstfruits, every dish in the house was scrubbed to be certain no leaven remained from previous meals. Only after this cleansing was complete, could the women begin to prepare for the feasts.

The feast of Unleavened Bread continued for seven days. It symbolized a time of putting away of sin – of becoming separate from sin – of being consecrated to God.

Leaven is always a type of sin, of false doctrine, or deception. The preparational cleansing speaks of the fact that it takes very little leaven to affect the whole.

This feast portrayed the perfect sinless sacrifice of Jesus. The apostle Paul explained the importance of this sacrifice to us.

1 Corinthians 5:7,8 Therefore purge out the old leaven, that you may be a new lump, since you truly are unleavened. For indeed Christ, our Passover, was sacrificed for us. Therefore let us keep the feast, not with old leaven, nor with the leaven of malice and wickedness, but with the unleavened bread of sincerity and truth.

Feast of Harvest or First Fruits (Bikkurin)

Reference: Leviticus 23:9-14

The feast of First Fruits was started when the children of Israel entered into the Promised Land. There was no sowing and reaping as they wandered in the wilderness.

This feast, celebrated in the spring, centered around waving a sheaf of the first fruits of the harvest before Jehovah. The first fruit always represented the best. This one sheaf represented the whole harvest and was a time of giving thanks to God for the harvest which was to come.

The apostle Paul referred to Jesus as the First-Fruit of the resurrection.

1 Corinthians 15:20,21 But now Christ is risen from the dead, and has become the firstfruits of those who have fallen asleep. For since by man came death, by Man also came the resurrection of the dead.

When Jesus entered into heaven, He represented all of those who were to follow Him in resurrection. Jesus is the First-Fruit and we are the harvest.

Feast of Pentecost (Shavuot)

References: Exodus 19,20,24; Exodus 23:16,17; Leviticus 23:15-21; Numbers 28:26-31; Deuteronomy 16:9-12

When Moses first went to Pharaoh, he asked that the children of Israel be allowed to go into the wilderness to hold a feast. When they were set free and came to Mount Sinai, they set up camp. While they were there, the Lord gave them the Law and the Feast of Pentecost. It was first celebrated fifty days after leaving Egypt.

The offering for the Feast of Pentecost was two loaves of bread. The crushing and milling of the wheat pictured the suffering and death of Jesus from which came two loaves – the Old Testament believers and the New Testament believers.

The Old Testament believers depended on the future death of Christ for their redemption. They depended on His resurrection for their transference from Paradise to Heaven. Their faith always was in the coming Messiah. Our faith looks back.

The Feast of Pentecost represented the infilling of the Holy Spirit. It was fulfilled on the day of Pentecost when the Holy Spirit was poured out on mankind.

Acts 2:1-4 Now when the Day of Pentecost had fully come, they were all with one accord in one place. And suddenly there came a sound from heaven, as of a rushing mighty wind, and it filled the whole house where they were sitting. Then there appeared to them divided tongues, as of fire, and one sat upon each of them. And they were all filledwith the Holy Spirit and began to speak with other tongues, as the Spirit gave them utterance.

With the coming of the Holy Spirit, the Law was taken from being written in stone to being written on our hearts. The apostle Paul and the writer of the book of Hebrews explains this.

2 Corinthians 3:2,3 You are our epistle written in our hearts, known and read by all men; clearly you are an epistle of Christ, ministered by us, written not with ink but by the Spirit of the living God, not on tablets of stone but on tablets of flesh, that is, of the heart.

Hebrews 10:15,16 And the Holy Spirit also witnesses to us; for after He had said before, this is the covenant that I will make with them after those days, says the LORD: I will put My laws into their hearts, and in their minds I will write them.

Feast of Trumpets (Rosh Hashana)

Reference: Leviticus 23:23-25

To understand the Feast of Trumpets, we must first understand the use of trumpets both in the Old and New Testaments. When Moses came down from Mount Sinai, the people consecrated themselves and then we read,

Exodus 19:16 Then it came to pass on the third day, in the morning, that there were thunderings and lightnings, and a thick cloud on the mountain; and the sound of the trumpet was very loud, so that all the people who were in the camp trembled.

The people didn't tremble at the sound of the thunderings or at the lightnings, or even at the thick cloud that rested on the mountain. They trembled at the sound of the loud trumpet which could be heard over the thunder.

The trumpets had a loud clarion call that could be heard over the tumult of battle, and across the land.

The trumpets were used to call the people to worship. Over and over again, the sound of the trumpets was heard throughout the land of Israel. They declared, *"Come and worship the Lord."*

The trumpets were heard as a call to battle, to sound the advance, to celebrate the victory.

Jeremiah wrote,

Jeremiah 51:27 Set up a banner in the land, blow the trumpet among the nations!

The sound of the trumpet was a declaration.

Isaiah wrote,

Isaiah 58:1 Cry aloud, spare not; lift up your voice like a trumpet; tell My people their transgression, and the house of Jacob their sins.

The sounds of trumpets had meaning. In the book of Revelation, trumpets and voices were used with almost the same meaning.

Trumpets signify prophecy – speaking out the word of God.

Today, the Feast of Trumpets is a call to harvest. We celebrate it by declaring God's Word to those around us, to our own nation, and to the nations of the world. The sound of the trumpet is the voice of believers declaring Jesus is the Son of God – that He came in the flesh for our salvation – that all who accept Him can become the sons of God.

Believers are to fulfill this feast every day, but there is still coming a final fulfillment. There will be a final trumpet call. The apostle wrote about this.

1 Corinthians 15:51-54 Behold, I tell you a mystery: We shall not all sleep, but we shall all be changed–In a moment, in the twinkling of an eye, at the last trumpet.

For the trumpet will sound, and the dead will be raised incorruptible, and we shall be changed.

For this corruptible must put on incorruption, and this mortal must put on immortality. So when this corruptible has put on incorruption, and this mortal has put on immortality, then shall be brought to pass the saying that is written: "Death is swallowed up in victory."

Jesus died on the Day of Passover becoming the fulfillment of the Passover. The Holy Spirit came on the Day of Pentecost fulfilling that feast. Many believe that Jesus will return on the Feast of Trumpets since that feast is still unfulfilled.

Day of Atonement (Yom Kippur)

Reference: Leviticus 23:26-32

The Day of Atonement was the most wonderful, sacred feast of the whole year. It was the one time each year the high priest could go into the Holy of Holies to make sacrifice for the people.

➢ *The Shed Blood*

Atonement means the covering of sins by the blood of the lamb. It looked forward to the remission of sins by the blood of Jesus – the perfect Lamb of God.

On the day of atonement each year, the high priest shed the blood of an innocent lamb without spot or blemish. This blood was carried within the veil and sprinkled on the mercy seat as a covering for the sins of the people.

The shedding of the blood of the innocent lamb represented the substitutionary sacrifice of Jesus on the cross. Jesus, the lamb of God, shed His blood and redeemed us from the slavery and penalty of sin.

Under the Old Covenant, this sacrifice and sprinkling of blood provided an atonement, or covering, for the sins of the people who by faith, looked forward to the cross. The Old Testament believers, like Abraham, believed God and it was counted unto them for righteousness.

Under the New Covenant, the word atonement or covering is no longer used. Based on the completed work of Christ's great eternal sacrifice, our sins are no longer covered, they have been remitted (passed over), borne away, removed, canceled. They cease to exist.

Psalms 103:12 As far as the east is from the west, so far has He removed our transgressions from us.

➢ *The Scapegoat*

This removal of our transgressions was represented by the second innocent lamb on the Day of Atonement. This was the scapegoat upon whom the high priest imparted the transgressions of the people by the laying on of hands. The scapegoat was then led away into the wilderness and released. This was a type of the bearing away of the sins of the people by the coming Lamb of God.

Leviticus 16:10,21,22 But the goat on which the lot fell to be the scapegoat shall be presented alive before the LORD, to make atonement upon it, and to let it go as the scapegoat into the wilderness. ... and Aaron shall lay both his hands on the head of the live goat, confess over it all the iniquities of the children of Israel, and all their transgressions, concerning all their sins, putting them on the head of the goat, and shall send it away into the wilderness by the hand of a suitable man. The goat shall bear on itself all their iniquities to an uninhabited land; and he shall release the goat in the wilderness.

Even as the sacrificial lamb on the Day of Atonement was a type of the substitutionary work of Jesus, even so was the work of the scapegoat as the sins of the people were borne away.

John 1:29b ... Behold! The lamb of God who takes away the sin of the world!

Jesus became our sacrifice by His death on the cross. Jesus also bore our sins away. This bearing away of our sins was a part of making atonement

> *Our Substitute*

The substitutionary work of Jesus was prophesied by Isaiah.

Isaiah 53:8-12 He was taken from prison and from judgment, and who will declare His generation? For He was cut off from the land of the living; for the transgressions of My people He was stricken. And they made His grave with the wicked–but with the rich at His death, because He had done no violence, nor was any deceit in His mouth. Yet it pleased the LORD to bruise Him; He has put Him to grief.

When You make His soul an offering for sin, He shall see His seed, He shall prolong His days, and the pleasure of the LORD shall prosper in His hand. He shall see the travail of His soul, and be satisfied. by His knowledge My righteous Servant shall justify many, for He shall bear their iniquities.

Therefore I will divide Him a portion with the great, and He shall divide the spoil with the strong, because He poured out His soul unto death, and He was numbered with the transgressors, and He bore the sin of many, and made intercession for the transgressors.

David also foretold this time when Jesus would bear away our sins to the depth of the lowest pit.

Psalms 88:3-7 For my soul is full of troubles, and my life draws near to the grave. I am counted with those who go down to the pit; I am like a man who has no strength, adrift among the dead, like the slain who lie in the grave, whom You remember no more, and who are cut off from Your hand. You have laid me in the lowest pit, in darkness, in the depths. Your wrath lies heavy upon me, and You have afflicted me with all Your waves.

Our iniquities had been subdued.

Micah 7:19 He will again have compassion on us, and will subdue our iniquities. You will cast all our sins into the depths of the sea.

Having borne our sins away to the depths of the earth where they were totally subdued, destroyed, remitted and ceased to exist, Jesus arose from the dead and ascended to the Father bearing His blood to be deposited within the veil in heaven. At that moment, our redemption was a completed work.

Hebrews 9:11,12 But Christ came as High Priest of the good things to come, with the greater and more perfect tabernacle not made with hands, that is, not of this creation. Not with the blood of goats and calves, but with His own blood He entered the Most Holy Place once for all, having obtained eternal redemption.

➢ Through His sacrifice, our salvation was complete.
➢ Through Him, we have forgiveness for our sins.
➢ Through Him, we are free from the penalties of sin.

Jesus' work to provide for the remission of our sins is complete. As we live, we accept it by faith.

The Day of Atonement looks forward to the future day when national Israel shall recognize Jesus as their Messiah, and shall mourn for Him, as one mourns for an only son.

Zechariah 12:10 And I will pour on the house of David and on the inhabitants of Jerusalem the Spirit of grace and supplication; then they will look on Me whom they have pierced; they will mourn for Him as one mourns for his only son, and grieve for Him as one grieves for a firstborn.

Feast of Tabernacles (Succoth)

Reference: Leviticus 23:33-44; Deuteronomy 16:13,14; Nehemiah 8:13-18

The Feast of Tabernacles celebrated the children of Israel entering into the promised land. For seven days they moved out of their homes and lived in booths made of palm branches and other leafy boughs tied with willow saplings. It was a time of remembering the wanderings in the wilderness and rejoicing over the fact that God had brought them into their own land.

The Feast of Trumpets was held at harvest time. On the last day of the feast, Jesus stood in the temple and declared,

John 7:37b "If anyone thirsts, let him come to Me and drink."

The Feast of Tabernacles is a picture of our life in Christ. It is a time of rest in Him. It is a time of living in permanent homes, and yet, remembering our time here is temporary. It is a time of living in the natural (the land), and yet, of living in the Spirit.

It is a picture of the rest to be enjoyed by the believers during the Millennium – one without battles or strife. The Jewish nation looks forward to this as their final *"kingdom"* rest. It represents the seventh day rest – the day when the Lord's kingdom rules over all the earth.

Some believers stop at the Feast of Passover with salvation. Others go on to experience Pentecost. There is still more, there is an entering into the land, an establishing of God's kingdom on this earth.

For us, it is a time of taking our promised inheritance, walking in dominion, and forcefully advancing the kingdom of God on this earth.

KINGS AND PRIESTS FOREVER

Our Spiritual Sacrifices
➤ *Our Bodies*

Romans 12:1 I beseech you therefore, brethren, by the mercies of God, thast you present your bodies a living sacrifice, holy, acceptable to God, which is your reasonable service.

➤ *Our Giving*

Phil. 4:18 Indeed I have all and abound, I am full, having received from Epaphroditus the things which were sent from you, a sweet-smelling aroma, an acceptable sacrifice, well pleasing to God.

➤ *Praise*

Hebrews 13:15 Therefore by Him let us continually offer the sacrifice of praise to God, that is, the fruit of our lips, giving thanks to His name.

Ps. 116:17 I will offer to You the sacrifice of thanksgiving, and will call upon the name of the LORD.

➤ *Lifting Hands*

Ps. 141:2 Let my prayer be set before You as incense, the lifting up of my hands as the evening sacrifice.

➤ *Righteousness*

Ps. 4:5 Offer the sacrfices of righteousness, and put your trust in the LORD.

➤ *Joy*

Ps. 27:6 And now my head shall be lifted up above my enmies all around me; therefore I will offer sacrifices of joy in His tabernacle; I will sing, yes, I will sing prasies to the LORD.

➤ *Broken Spirit and Contrite Heart*

Ps. 51:17 The sacrifiecs of God are a broken spirit, a broken and a contrite heart – these, O God, You will not despise.

The ministry of the kings and priests of the Old Testament is important for us to understand, because all believers today have been made kings and priests.

Revelation 1:5,6 And from Jesus Christ, the faithful witness, the firstborn from the dead, and the ruler over the kings of the earth. To Him who loved us and washed us from our sins in His own blood, and has made us kings and priests to His God and Father, to Him be glory and dominion forever and ever. Amen.

As king-priests, we have ministry functions to perform. As kings we are to live in dominion over this earth, to forcibly advance God's kingdom on this earth. We are to exercise our restored spiritual authority and pull down strongholds over people's lives and the governments of this world. We are to reign in this life as kings.

Romans 5:17 For if by the one man's offense death reigned through the one, much more those who receive abundance of grace and of the gift of righteousness will reign in life through the One, Jesus Christ.

We reign as kings through our witness, world evangelism, and mission outreaches. He has given us the nations for our inheritance.

Psalm 111:6 He has declared to His people the power of His works, in giving them the heritage of the nations.

When Jesus returns to this earth to set up His kingdom, we will reign with Him on this earth for one thousand years.

Revelation 2:26,27a And he who overcomes, and keeps My works until the end, to him I will give power over the nations– He shall rule them with a rod of iron ...

1 Corinthians 6:2,3 Do you not know that the saints will judge the world? And if the world will be judged by you, are you unworthy to judge the smallest matters? Do you not know that we shall judge angels? How much more, things that pertain to this life?

As priests, we have functions to perform as His representatives to mankind. We are to offer the sacrifice of praise to God continually. We are to minister to the Lord through sacrificial giving. We are to be God's priestly representatives to the lost of this world.

The priestly ministry of the Levitical priesthood is a type of our priestly ministry as believer-priests today.

Levitical Priesthood

When the children of Israel were led out of Egypt and God gave them the Law, the tribe of Levi was separated out to be the priests. There were many priests, but there was only one high priest at a time. These men were priests because they were born into the family of Levi. They weren't individually selected as priests by God.

The high priests represented Jesus. We don't have space to go into his garments, but there is a rich study in every item that he wore.

It was the high priest who went into the Holy of Holies on the Day of Atonement and sprinkled the blood of the sacrifice on the mercy seat for the sins of all the people. The writer of the book of Hebrews has summarized this time for us.

Hebrews 9:7 But into the second part the high priest went alone once a year, not without blood, which he offered for himself and for the people's sins committed in ignorance.

From the time the Law was given, the descendants of Levi were ordained to be priests. However, when Jesus came, He was not a descendent of Aaron. He was not of the tribe of Levi. He was of the tribe of Judah – of David, and we are told He was a priest after the order of Melchizedek. Why?

The Levitical priesthood was a priesthood of acts – of doing – of works. It was a priesthood of men fulfilling the functions of the Law. The writer of the book of Hebrews said they were *"after the law of a fleshly commandment."*

Hebrews 7:16 (Jesus) Who has come, not according to the law of a fleshly commandment, but according to the power of an endless life.

The word *"fleshly"* means of the flesh – temporary. They were priests for a temporary time. The sacrifices they made for the sins of the people were for a temporary time. They had to be made again and again.

After the Order of Melchizedek

➤ *Who Was Melchizedek?*

The first mention of Melchizedek was in Genesis 14.

Genesis 14:18-20 Then Melchizedek king of Salem brought out bread and wine; he was the priest of God Most High. And he blessed him and said: "Blessed be Abram of God Most High, possessor of heaven and earth; and blessed be God Most High, Who has delivered your enemies into your hand." And he (Abram) gave him a tithe of all.

Melchizedek was a king and a priest. The writer of the book of Hebrews tells us much more about this meeting and who Melchizedek was.

Hebrews 7:1-3 For this Melchizedek, king of Salem, priest of the Most High God, who met Abraham returning from the slaughter of the kings and blessed him, to whom also Abraham gave a tenth part of all, first being translated "king of righteousness," and then also king of Salem, meaning "king of peace," without father, without mother, withoutgenealogy, having neither beginning of days nor end of life, but made like the Son of God, remains a priest continually.

Melchizedek was without a father, a mother, or a genealogy, having neither beginning or end. For this reason many feel Melchizedek was a theophany – an appearance of Christ in the Old Testament.

➤ *How Great Was He?*

The greatness of Melchizedek is measured by the fact that Abraham, chosen of God to be the father of a great family, the holder of the promise of the coming Messiah, a man of tremendous wealth, received a blessing from him. And in Abraham, all the coming priests of Levi received from a

Abraham, all the coming priests of Levi received from a greater priesthood. Again, we refer to the writing of Hebrews.

Hebrews 7:4-7 Now consider how great this man was, to whom even the patriarch Abraham gave a tenth of the spoils. And indeed those who are of the sons of Levi, who receive the priesthood, have a commandment to receive tithes from the people according to the law, that is, from their brethren, though they have come from the loins of Abraham; but he whose genealogy is not derived from them received tithes from Abraham and blessed him who had the promises. Now beyond all contradiction the lesser is blessed by the better.

Prophecy of David

David prophesied concerning the priesthood of Melchizedek. Notice, that this priest was chosen by God – sworn – and was a priest forever.

Psalms 110:4 The LORD has sworn and will not relent, "You are a priest forever according to the order of Melchizedek."

Confirmed in Hebrews

This prophecy was confirmed by the writer of the book of Hebrews.

Hebrews 5:6-10 As He also says in another place: "You are a priest forever according to the order of Melchizedek"; Who, in the days of His flesh, when He had offered up prayers and supplications, with vehement cries and tears to Him who was able to save Him from death, and was heard because of His godly fear, Though He was a Son, yet He learned obedience by the things which He suffered.

And having been perfected, He became the author of eternal salvation to all who obey Him, Called by God as High Priest "according to the order of Melchizedek."

A Change of Priesthood and Law

When Jesus died and was resurrected, the functions of the Levitical priesthood were complete. The sacrifice that He made was complete. There was no longer any need for the Levitical priesthood or for the sacrifices they made.

Hebrews 7:11,12 Therefore, if perfection were through the Levitical priesthood (for under it the people received the law), what further need was there that another priest should rise according to the order of Melchizedek, and not be called according to the order of Aaron? For the priesthood being changed, of necessity there is also a change of the law.

But the priesthood after the order of Melchizedek is eternal. The sacrifice is eternal.

Hebrews 7:24-27 But He, because He continues forever, has an unchangeable priesthood. Therefore He is also able to save to the uttermost those who come to God through Him, since He ever lives to make intercession for them. For such a High Priest was fitting for us, who is holy, harmless, undefiled, separate from sinners, and has become higher than the heavens; Who does not need daily, as those high priests, to offer up sacrifices, first for His own sins and then for the people's, for this He did once for all when He offered up Himself.

Priests Today

The priests of the Old Testament period were shadows of the real Priest. Jesus completely fulfilled the priesthood. There is no need for priests to make sacrifices, or to go to God for us today.

In the book of Revelation, we find that we are kings and priests. We are to offer sacrifices in the Spirit. We are to rule and reign with Christ.

Revelation 1:6 And has made us kings and priests to His God and Father, to Him be glory and dominion forever and ever. Amen.

Revelation 17:14 "These will make war with the Lamb, and the Lamb will overcome them, for He is LORD of lords and King of kings; and those who are with Him are called, chosen, and faithful."

Jesus is the Lord, and believers are the lords.

Jesus is the King, and believers are the kings.

Note: For more study on the tabernacle, priesthood, offerings and priests, we recommend reading **Pattern for Living**, by Alex W. Ness.

QUESTIONS FOR REVIEW

1. List the seven feasts of Israel.

2. Describe the significance of the Feast of Trumpets.

3. What are our functions as kings and priests today?

Lesson Seven

Old Testament Leaders

The Old Testament is filled with heroes – men and women we should know and imitate. Nothing can take the place of reading the Bible account of their lives.

As we read the accounts of the lives of Old Testament heroes, we should ask ourselves, "What made their lives different from those around them? What should I learn from them?" What they did is important, but perhaps we can learn more from who they were.

The writer of the book of Hebrews gives us a wonderful "roll-call" of heroes in Hebrews 11. Over and over again he uses the words "by faith." Finally, he stopped with these words:

Hebrews 11:32-34 And what more shall I say? For the time would fail me to tell of Gideon and Barak and Samson and Jephthah, also of David and Samuel and the prophets: <u>Who through faith</u>
- subdued kingdoms,
- worked righteousness,
- obtained promises,
- stopped the mouths of lions,
- quenched the violence of fire,
- escaped the edge of the sword,
- out of weakness were made strong,
- became valiant in battle,
- turned to flight the armies of the aliens.

The common ingredient in the life of every Bible hero was faith. They were ordinary men and women with ordinary weaknesses. They rose above these weaknesses and lived by faith.

ENOCH – WALKED WITH GOD

Reference: Genesis 4:17,18;5:19-25;Jude 1:14

Never Died!

Enoch lived for 365 years in the period of time before the flood. He lived during a time when mankind was so depraved that they brought the judgment of God down on themselves and the earth in the flood. And yet, Enoch "walked with God."

Strength:
Intimacy with God

Genesis 5:24 And Enoch walked with God; and he was not, for God took him.

Enoch didn't die! He was walking on this earth and then he was gone. The writer of the book of Hebrews tells us that this happened through faith.

Hebrews 11:5a By faith Enoch was translated so that he did not see death, and was not found because God had translated him ...

According to the Bible, there were only two men – Enoch and Elijah – who didn't die.

Enoch's Prophecy

In the book of Jude, we are given the prophecy of Enoch which is still to be fulfilled. It's interesting that the only prophecy given by Enoch announced the Second Coming of Christ.

Jude 1:14 Now Enoch, the seventh from Adam, prophesied about these men also, saying, "Behold, the LORD comes with ten thousands of His saints"

NOAH – BUILDER OF THE ARK

Reference: Genesis 5:29;6-9

120 Years of Faith & Obedience

As he built the ark, Noah walked in faith and obedience for 120 years during the most wicked time on the face of the earth. The Bible tells us that everyone on earth was corrupt.

Strengths:
Perseverance
Intimacy with God

Weakness:
Drunkenness

Genesis 6:5 Then the LORD saw that the wickedness of man was great in the earth, and that every intent of the thoughts of his heart was only evil continually.

Even though Noah was surrounded with this wickedness, we read,

Genesis 6:9b Noah was a just man, perfect in his generations. Noah walked with God.

Noah walked so closely with God, that God could give him the plan for the ark which would bring salvation to his family, and to the animals.

Noah was a real person. He had to walk by faith just as we do. Year after year, for over seventy years, he worked building a strange building, which he believed would float when a great flood came covering all the earth. No one had ever seen a boat, and it is very likely no one had ever seen rain. How the people around must have scoffed and ridiculed him. It must have seemed that he had gone out of his mind.

Noah is an example of someone who knows he has heard from God, and despite all persecution and misunderstanding, continues to believe what God has said. Noah is an example of persistent faith.

His life is summed up by the writer of the book of Hebrews.

Hebrews 11:7 By faith Noah, being divinely warned of things not yet seen, moved with godly fear, prepared an ark for the saving of his household, by which he condemned the world and became heir of the righteousness which is according to faith.

ABRAHAM – THE SPIRITUAL PILGRIM

Reference: Genesis 12-25:10

Note: God changed Abram's name to Abraham when he was 99 years old. For simplicity, we are using the name Abraham.

Friend of God – Father of Nations

Books have been written about the life of Abraham. His faith and obedience through years of wandering are without parallel. We are allowed to share closely in his triumphs as well as his failures. Abraham was very human, and yet he was chosen by God to become the father of many nations.

The writer of the book of Hebrews sums up his life with these words:

Hebrews 11:8-11 By faith Abraham obeyed when he was called to go out to the place which he would afterward receive as an inheritance. And he went out, not knowing where he was going.

By faith he sojourned in the land of promise as in a foreign country, dwelling in tents with Isaac and Jacob, the heirs with him of the same promise; for he waited for the city which has foundations, whose builder and maker is God.

By faith Sarah herself also received strength to conceive seed, and she bore a child when she was past the age, because she judged Him faithful who had promised.

We often hear of the faith of Abraham, but it is good to notice that the writer of the book of Hebrews also mentions the faith of Sarah.

Through the prophet Isaiah, God tells us that Abraham was His friend.

Isaiah 41:8 But you, Israel, are My servant, Jacob, whom I have chosen, the descendants of Abraham My friend.

Strengths:
Obedience
Hospitality
Knew God's Ways
Interceeded for Others
Generosity
Weakness:
Fear (of death, because of Sarah's beauty)

Called By God

The Bible tells us nothing about Abraham's life except his genealogy, until the age of seventy when God spoke to him in the land of Ur and called him out of that land.

Genesis 12:1-3 Now the LORD had said to Abram: "Get out of your country, from your kindred and from your father's house, to a land that I will show you. I will make you a great nation; I will bless you and make your name great; and you shall be a blessing. I will bless those who bless you, and I will curse him who curses you; and in you all the families of the earth shall be blessed."

God's promise to Abraham was three-fold.
➢ He would give him a land.
➢ He would be the father of a great nation.
➢ Through him, all the families of the earth would be blessed.

As wonderful as these promises must have seemed, they didn't give any specifics. Abraham had a choice. He could believe God, leave everything he knew, and move into an area of uncertainty and a walk of faith, or he could stay where he was. His response was obedience and faith.

Genesis 12:4a So Abram departed as the LORD had spoken to him ...

God didn't tell Abraham, before he left Ur, that He was going to give him a certain land. Instead, he was required to walk in faith, traveling through the land of Canaan, going from place to place as a nomad.

God continuously blessed him and gave him great wealth, but he had no son – no heir. Finally, sixteen years after God had promised him he would be the father of a great nation, through Hagar he had a son, Ishmael.

All the Arabic people are descendants of Ishmael. But Ishmael was not the promised son through which all the nations of the earth would be blessed.

Isaac is Born

Another thirteen years passed, and then God renewed His promise to Abraham.

Genesis 17:1,4- 6 When Abram was ninety-nine years old, the LORD appeared to Abram and said to him, "I am Almighty God; walk before Me and be blameless. As for Me, behold, My covenant is with you, and you shall be a father of many nations. No longer shall your name be called Abram, but your name shall be Abraham; for I have made you a father of many nations. I will make you exceedingly fruitful; and I will make nations of you, and kings shall come from you."

Genesis 21:5 Now Abraham was one hundred years old when his son Isaac was born to him.

The name, Abraham, means father of a great multitude.

The Sacrifice

Abraham had continued to believe God and waited thirty years for Isaac to be born. But then when Isaac was still a young man, God spoke to Abraham again. The Jewish historian, Josephus, puts Isaac's age at about twenty-five.

Genesis 22:1,2 Now it came to pass after these things that God tested Abraham, and said to him, "Abraham!" And he said, "Here I am."

And He said, "Take now your son, your only son Isaac, whom you love, and go to the land of Moriah, and offer him there as a burnt offering on one of the mountains of which I shall tell you."

It is impossible to even begin to understand how Abraham must have felt. God ... his Friend ... after waiting all those years for the promised son ... his heir ... God now said sacrifice Isaac?

Faith and Obedience

What was Abraham's response? Still obedience and faith.

Genesis 22:3 So Abraham rose early in the morning and saddled his donkey, and took two of his young men with him, and Isaac his son; and he split the wood for the burnt offering, and arose and went to the place of which God had told him.

We see his faith when we read what he said to the young men as he left them.

Genesis 22:4,5 Then on the third day Abraham lifted his eyes and saw the place afar off. And Abraham said to his young men, "Stay here with the donkey; the lad and I will go yonder and worship, and we will come back to you."

We will come back to you. Abraham was going to make the sacrifice God required; but he still knew God had given him this promised son, and that he was going to be the father of many nations.

We hear his faith when he responded to Isaac.

Genesis 22:8a And Abraham said, "My son, God will provide for Himself the lamb for a burnt offering."

At the last minute, God did provide a substitute sacrifice.

Genesis 22:11-13 But the Angel of the LORD called to him from heaven and said, "Abraham, Abraham!"

And he said, "Here I am."

And He said, "Do not lay your hand on the lad, or do anything to him; for now I know that you fear God, seeing you have not withheld your son, your only son, from Me."

Then Abraham lifted his eyes and looked, and there behind him was a ram caught in a thicket by its horns. So Abraham went and took the ram, and offered it up for a burnt offering instead of his son.

In this sacrifice, we are given a wonderful picture of God the Father giving His Son as the Sacrifice for the whole world. If we went into a study of geography, we would see that it is very possible that the sacrifice of the substitute ram was made in the same place Jesus would be crucified hundreds of years later.

JACOB – FROM SUPPLANTER TO PRINCE

Reference: Genesis 25:21-49:33

From Jacob to Israel

Jacob's life is one of contrasts. His name meant supplanter, and his life started out as just that. And yet God said, *"Jacob have I loved."*

Strengths:
 Knew God's Ways

Weakness:
 Deceptive

His story is one of men and women trying to make God's plans happen. It is a story of people trying to work through the flesh what God would work in the spirit. It is also a wonderful example of the life-changing power of knowing God.

Before the twins Esau and Jacob were born, God spoke concerning them.

Genesis 25:23 And the LORD said to her: "Two nations are in your womb, two peoples shall be separated from your body; one people shall be stronger than the other, and the older shall serve the younger."

God had said, "The older shall serve the younger," but in Genesis 25, we see how Jacob persuaded Esau to give up his birthright for one meal. In Genesis 27, we read the story of how Rebekah and Jacob plotted to steal the birthright blessing from Esau, the older son. Jacob acted in deceit, lied to his father, and even used the Lord's name in his lies. He received the blessing meant for Esau, but then, in fear for his life, he had to flee.

Vision at Bethel

Even as Jacob was fleeing from his brother's wrath, he had a vision at Bethel.

Genesis 28:12-15 Then he dreamed, and behold, a ladder was set up on the earth, and its top reached to heaven; and there the angels of God were ascending and descending on it.

And behold, the LORD stood above it and said: "I am the LORD God of Abraham your father and the God of Isaac; the land on which you lie I will give to you and your descendants. Also your descendants shall be as the dust of the earth; you shall spread abroad to the west and the east, to the north and the south; and in you and in your seed all the families of the earth shall be blessed. Behold, I am with you and will keep you wherever you go, and will bring you back to this land; for I will not leave you until I have done what I have spoken to you."

God renewed the promise He had given to Abraham to Jacob. The Messiah would come through Jacob.

Genesis 28:20 Then Jacob made a vow, saying, "If God will be with me, and keep me in this way that I am going, and give me bread to eat and clothing to put on, so that I come back to my father's house in peace, then the LORD shall be my God. And this stone which I have set as a pillar shall be God's house, and of all that You give me I will surely give a tenth to You."

The Deceiver Deceived

Jacob's life didn't suddenly become perfect. He had deceived his father, and now he was deceived by Laban who would be his father-in-law. He made an agreement to work seven years for Rachel to be his wife, but Laban and Leah, Rachel's sister, deceived him and he had to work another seven years to pay for Rachel.

Finally, after Jacob had been with Laban for twenty turbulent years in which Laban continuously took advantage of him, God told him to return to his own land.

Genesis 31:13 I am the God of Bethel, where you anointed the pillar and where you made a vow to Me. Now arise, get out of this land, and return to the land of your kindred.

Jacob obeyed God, but he was still afraid of his brother Esau; and when he heard Esau was on the way to meet him with four-hundred men, he started praying! He reminded God of His promises to him. He prayed for protection for his wives and children.

Meeting at Peniel

As he continued to pray at Peniel, Jacob had a personal meeting with God. His name and his life were changed.

Genesis 32:24-30 Then Jacob was left alone; and a Man wrestled with him until the breaking of day. Now when He saw that He did not prevail against him, He touched the socket of his hip; and the socket of Jacob's hip was out of joint as He wrestled with him. And He said, "Let Me go, for the day breaks."

But he said, "I will not let You go unless You bless me!"

So He said to him, "What is your name?" And he said, "Jacob."

And He said, "Your name shall no longer be called Jacob, but Israel; for you have struggled with God and with men, and have prevailed."

Then Jacob asked Him, saying, "Tell me Your name, I pray."

And He said, "Why is it that you ask about My name?" And He blessed him there.

And Jacob called the name of the place Peniel: "For I have seen God face to face, and my life is preserved."

Jacob, the supplanter, had become Israel, the Soldier of God. His descendants were known as the children of Israel, or Israelites. They are still known by that name.

> **Is it permissible to struggle with God?**
> *Yes, if it is done in faith with proper motivations*
>
> **Examples are:**
> *Abraham struggled with God for Sodom and Gomorrah*
> *Jacob struggled with God for a blessing*
> *Moses struggled with God for the children of Israel*

JOSEPH – A SAVIOR OF NATIONS

Reference: Genesis 37-50

From Riches to Rags – Twice

From the Bible account of Joseph's life, his childhood seemed idyllic. His father, Jacob, was very wealthy and Joseph was his favorite son. As a child, Joseph even heard from God in specific dreams.

These dreams, his favored status with their father, and perhaps, his pride, earned him the hatred of his brothers. They cast him into a pit and then sold him into slavery.

Genesis 37:28 Then Midianite traders passed by; so the brothers pulled Joseph up and lifted him out of the pit, and sold him to the Ishmaelites for twenty shekels of silver. And they took Joseph to Egypt.

In Egypt, Joseph became the overseer of Potiphar, a wealthy man's house and goods. He had risen to a position of honor for a slave. But then, Potiphar's wife tried to get him to sin with her.

> **Strengths:**
> *Forgiving heart*
> *Creative, organized mind*
> *Pleasant personality*
> *Servant's heart*
>
> **Weakness:**
> *Pride – boasted of dreams to his family*

Genesis 39:7-9 Now it came to pass after these things that his master's wife cast longing eyes on Joseph, and she said, "Lie with me."

But he refused and said to his master's wife, "Look, my master does not know what is with me in the house, and he has committed all that he has to my hand. There is no one greater in this house than I, nor has he kept back anything from me but you, because you are his wife. How then can I do this great wickedness, and sin against God?"

Because Joseph wouldn't be seduced, Potiphar's wife accused him falsely and he was thrown into prison.

Genesis 39:19,20 So it was, when his master heard the words which his wife spoke to him, saying, "Your servant did to me after this manner," that his anger was aroused. Then Joseph's master took him and put him into the prison, a place where the king's prisoners were confined. And he was there in the prison.

Joseph had gone from being the favored son to being an honored slave. Now, he was a prisoner. His earlier dreams must have seemed far away. He must have wondered if God had given those dreams to him. Symbolically, he had seen his brothers bowing down to him, but now he was a slave in prison. He might well have asked, *"God, what am I doing wrong?"*

Joseph, however, continued to hear from God and interpreted dreams for others in the prison. Then God gave Pharaoh a dream, and no one could explain it – no one except Joseph. He was brought from the prison and God gave him its interpretation. Through the dream and its interpretation of a coming famine, Joseph became second to Pharaoh.

The famine came just as Joseph had predicted and the people of many tribes came to Egypt for the food which had been stored at Joseph's commands. Joseph's brothers were among those that came. And they did bow down to him just as he had dreamed.

> **Did God let Joseph be sold into slavery and cast into prison for no reason?**
>
> *When God has a great plan for our lives, there are "learning periods" we must go through. God had to bring discipline into Joseph's life so that he could handle the responsibilites of rulership.*

Lessons to Learn

What should we learn from Joseph's life?

When God gives us a dream or vision, He will bring it to pass. Sometimes, we don't see God's timing, and the hard places in our life may be to change us to be a person God can use, and to move us to the place where God needs us.

Joseph is also a wonderful example of forgiveness working in the life of a believer.

A Type of Christ

Joseph is an Old Testament type of Christ.
➤ He left his position of wealth and went to a distant land.
➤ He brought salvation to the nations.
➤ He freely forgave his brothers.

Joseph summed up all he had been through with these words,

Genesis 50:19,20 Joseph said to them, "Do not be afraid, for am I in the place of God? But as for you, you meant evil against me; but God meant it for good, in order to bring it about as it is this day, to save many people alive."

MOSES – DELIVERER FROM BONDAGE

Reference: Exodus – Deuteronomy

40 Years in Pharaoh's Household

Moses was born a slave, put into a basket on the river Nile by his mother to save his life, and was found by Pharaoh's daughter. He was raised as a son of Pharaoh, but when the time came, he identified with his people. The writer of the book of Hebrews explains this.

Hebrews 11:24-27 By faith Moses, when he became of age, refused to be called the son of Pharaoh's daughter, choosing rather to suffer affliction with the people of God than to enjoy the passing pleasures of sin, esteeming the reproach of Christ greater riches than the treasures in Egypt; for he looked to the reward. By faith he forsook Egypt, not fearing the wrath of the king; for he endured as seeing Him who is invisible.

40 Years Hidden in the Desert

Strengths:
Meekness
Knew God's ways

Weaknesses:
A bad temper that caused impulsive acts:
Killed an Egyptian
Fought the shepherds
Broke the tables of stone
Struck the rock a second time

Moses fled to the desert and spent forty years of his life there. Then God appeared to him in the burning bush and called him to bring his people out of slavery.

Exodus 3:2,4,6,9,10 And the Angel of the LORD appeared to him in a flame of fire from the midst of a bush. So he looked, and behold, the bush burned with fire, but the bush was not consumed. ... So when the LORD saw that he turned aside to look, God called to him from the midst of the bush and said, "Moses, Moses!"

And he said, "Here I am."

Moreover He said, "I am the God of your father–the God of Abraham, the God of Isaac, and the God of Jacob." And Moses hid his face, for he was afraid to look upon God.

"Now therefore, behold, the cry of the children of Israel has come to Me, and I have also seen the oppression with which the Egyptians oppress them. Come now, therefore, and I will send you to Pharaoh that you may bring My people, the children of Israel, out of Egypt."

40 Years – Leader of Children of Israel

There can be no greater example of a person moving in God's authority than Moses. He brought the plagues on Pharaoh's house. He held up his rod and the sea parted. He threw a tree into the bitter water and it became sweet. He talked with God. He even argued with God for the lives of his people. He led a tribe of over a million people through the desert for forty years. Through him, we were given the tabernacle and the Law. And yet, we read in Numbers that Moses was very humble – more humble than all men who were on the face of the earth.

Numbers 12:3 (Now the man Moses was very humble, more than all men who were on the face of the earth.)

What leadership quality can we learn from Moses? True humility and authority. God's authority operates through humble people. Humility is not thinking of yourself without pride. It is not thinking of yourself at all.

Moses is the only man who was buried by God.

Deuteronomy 34:4-7 Then the LORD said to him, "This is the land of which I swore to give Abraham, Isaac, and Jacob, saying, `I will give it to your descendants.' I have caused you to see it with your eyes, but you shall not cross over there." So Moses the servant of the LORD died there in the land of Moab, according to the word of the LORD. And He buried him in a valley in the land of Moab, opposite Beth Peor; but no one knows his grave to this day. Moses was one hundred and twenty years old when he died. His eyes were not dim nor his natural vigor abated.

DAVID – GREATEST KING OF ISRAEL

David is one of the most prominent figures throughout history. The nation of Israel reached its greatest size during his reign. David is prominent in four books of the Old Testament – 1 and 2 Samuel, 1 Chronicles, and the Psalms. Because of his importance in history, Jesus was not referred to as the Son of Abraham, but rather, as the Son of David.

His Anointing

David was the youngest of eight sons, but while he was still tending the sheep in his father's household, God sent Samuel to anoint him to be the next king of Israel.

1 Samuel 16:12b,13 And the LORD said, "Arise, anoint him; for this is the one!" Then Samuel took the horn of oil and anointed him in the midst of his brothers; and the Spirit of the LORD came upon David from that day forward.

Immediately, David was called to the house of King Saul to play his harp. We don't know how long he remained in that position. We do know he had returned home before the time of his meeting with the giant Goliath.

His Courage

David was a person of courage beginning with the time he killed the lion and the bear while taking care of his father's sheep.

Strengths:

Was a worshiper
Had respect for anointing
Knew God's ways
Accepted correction and repented

Weakness:

Beautiful women
Failure to discipline familyand close friends

1 Samuel 17:34,35 But David said to Saul, "Your servant used to keep his father's sheep, and when a lion or a bear came and took a lamb out of the flock, I went out after it and struck it, and delivered the lamb from its mouth; and when it arose against me, I caught it by its beard, and struck and killed it."

David had tested his faith in God, and his courage in these incidents, and they gave him the faith he needed to kill the giant Goliath.

1 Samuel 17:26 Then David spoke to the men who stood by him, saying, "What shall be done for the man who kills this Philistine and takes away the reproach from Israel? For who is this uncircumcised Philistine, that he should defy the armies of the living God?"

1 Samuel 17:45-47 Then David said to the Philistine, "You come to me with a sword, with a spear, and with a javelin. But I come to you in the name of the LORD of hosts, the God of the armies of Israel, whom you have defied. This day the LORD will deliver you into my hand, and I will strike you and take your head from you. And this day I will give the carcasses of the camp of the Philistines to the birds of the air and the wild beasts of the earth, that all the earth may know that there is a God in Israel. Then all this assembly shall know that the LORD does not save with sword and spear; for the battle is the LORD'S, and He will give you into our hands."

We know the rest of the story. David couldn't wear the king's armor, but instead went against the giant with five small stones and a slingshot. He killed the giant and became a hero to all the people.

His Forbearance

David had been anointed the next king of Israel by God while he was a lowly shepherd. How providential it must have seemed as he was moved from that position to being Saul's harpist, then his general, and finally his son-in-law. He even became best friends with Jonathan, Saul's son and the natural heir to the throne.

But Saul became jealous of him and afraid of his popularity with the people. Saul could see that he could easily become the next king and he tried to kill him several times. David ran for his life and lived in caves as an outlaw. He could have killed Saul two different times, but he refused to do so.

1 Samuel 24:10 " Look, this day your eyes have seen that the LORD delivered you today into my hand in the cave, and someone urged me to kill you. But my eye spared you, and I said, `I will not stretch out my hand against my LORD, for he is the LORD'S anointed.' "

1 Samuel 26:8,9 Then Abishai said to David, "God has delivered your enemy into your hand this day. Now therefore, please, let me strike him at once with the spear, right to the earth; and I will not have to strike him a second time!" And David said to Abishai, "Do not destroy him; for who can stretch out his hand against the LORD'S anointed, and be guiltless?"

Saul died and David was made the king of Judah. Then Saul's son died and David became king of all Israel.

His Reign

➤ There were many notable events during David's reign as king. He captured Jerusalem and made it the capitol of Israel.
➤ He brought the ark to Jerusalem establishing the tabernacle of David.
➤ He enlarged the kingdom.
➤ He took Bathsheba, the wife of Uriah, and then repented of his sin publicly.
➤ He was given the plans for the great temple which was built by his son Solomon.

A Worshiper of God

David's greatest legacy to us was as a skilled musician. He was a worshiper of God. He wrote the greatest percentage of the book of Psalms which are the most encouraging words for discouraged, distressed or troubled believers today. He wrote the most marvelous prophecies of the coming Messiah.

Through the tabernacle of David, he gave us a wonderful picture of what praise and worship should be today.

David was a warrior, a king, a prophet, and a psalmist. He was a man after God's own heart.

Acts 13:22 And when He had removed him, He raised up for them David as king, to whom also He gave testimony and said, `I have found David the son of Jesse, a man after My own heart, who will do all My will.'

Summary

There is not enough space to go on into the lives of Joshua – the Soldier of the Lord, Gideon – the Mighty Man of Valor, Samuel – the Upright Judge, or Solomon, Elijah, Elisha, Daniel, Ezra, or Nehemiah. There is no space to study Sarah, Esther, Ruth, or Deborah. But everywhere we look throughout the Old Testament period, God had a man or a woman to fulfill His will. There was always a hero that would stand up and be counted for the Lord.

These heroes were real men and women who had strengths and weaknesses just as we have. When we appreciate them as real people, we can see ourselves doing the things they id. We can see ourselves being the Gideon or Deborah of our time.

QUESTIONS FOR REVIEW

1. What was the common ingredient in the life of every Old Testament Bible hero listed in Hebrews 11?

2. Give biblical examples of the obedience and faith of Abraham.

3. In what ways was Joseph a type of Christ?

Miracles of the Old Testament
(A Partial List)

Creation	**Genesis**
Of Earth	Ch 1
Of Humanity	1:26,27
	2:7,21,22

Enoch's Translation 5:19-24

The Flood 7:9-12,17-24

Tower of Babel 11:1.5-9

Abraham

Plague on Pharaoh and His House	12:10-20
Smoking Furnace and Burning Lamp	15:17,18
Sarah's Conception	17:15-19
	18:10-14;21:1-3
Blinded Sodomites	19:9-11
Destruction of Sodom and Gomorrah	19:15-25,28,29
Lot's Wife Turned to Salt	19:24-28
Hagar's Well	21:14-21

Moses	**Exodus**
Burning Bush	3:1-14
Rod of Moses	4:1-5;7:8-13
Leprous Hand	4:6-12

Ten Plagues on Egypt

Nile River	4:9,14-24
Frogs	8:1-6
Lice	8:16-19
Flies	8:20-31
Pestilence on Animals	9:1-7
Boils	9:8-11
Hail	9:13-25
Locust	10:1-20
Darkness	10:21-29
Death of Firstborn	Ch 11;12:29-33

Journey Through Wilderness

The Cloud and Fire	13:21 and on
Parting of Red Sea	14:21-31
Marah's Healing Waters	15:22-27
Manna	16:1-5 and on
Quails	16:8,11-13
Water from Rock	17:1-9
Victory over Amalek	17:8-16
At Sinai : Fire - thick cloud	19:16-25
lightning – thunder – earthquake	Deut. 5:22-26
voice of trumpet – writing of ten commandments	

Judgment on Nadab and Abihu .... Leviticus 10:1-7

	Numbers
Murmurers Consumed by Fire	11:1-3
Miriam's Leprosy	Ch 12;20:1

Destruction of Korah and Others	Ch 16;26:9-11
Aaron's Rod	Ch 17
Brazen Serpent	21:4-9
Well at Beer	21:13-18
Balaam's Ass	22:20-35
Victory over Midianites	Ch 25;31
Moses' Burial	Deuteronomy 34

Joshua	**Joshua**
Parting of Jordan River	3:7-17:4
Miraculous Appearance	5:13-15
Taking of Jericho	Ch 6
Sun Stood Still	10:12-15

Gideon	**Judges**
Fire Came from Rock	6:19-24
The Fleece	6:36-40
Midian's Defeat	Ch 7

Elijah	**1 Kings**
Long drought	17:1; James 5:17
Fed by Ravens	17:2-7
Resurrection of Widow's Son	17:17-24
Miraculous Sacrifice	18:1-39
Miraculous Rain	18:1,2
Angelic Meal	19:1-18
Divine Manifestation	19:9-18

	2 Kings
Fire from Heaven	1:9-15
Parting of Jordan	2:1-8
Elijah Taken in Chariots of Fire	2:9-11

Elisha

Parting of Jordan	2:12-14
Healed Waters	2:19-22
Judgment of Irreverence	2:23-25
Flooded Ditches	3:1-22
Widow's Oil	4:1-7
Resurrection of Shunammite's Son	4:8-37
Naaman's Healing	5:1-19
Gehazi's Leprosy	5:26,27
Floating Axhead	6:1-7
Blinded and Opened Eyes	6:8-23

Jonah	**Jonah**
Swallowed Unharmed by Great Fish	1:17;2:10

Daniel	**Daniel**
Saved from Lions' Den	6:16-23
Revealer of Dreams	2:15-23

Shadrach, Meshach, Abed-nego

Saved from Fiery Furnace	3:19-29

Lesson Eight

Miracles of Creation and Judgment

A miracle is a supernatural intervention in the laws of nature to accommodate God's purposes in either bringing supernatural blessing for obedience or judgment for disobedience.

MIRACLES OF CREATION

Of Heaven and Earth
➢ *God Spoke*

The creation of the heavens and the earth is a wonderful example of the mighty miracle working power of God. He spoke and it was done! The Genesis account of creation uses the words, *"He spoke"* over and over. David and the writer of the book of Hebrews used the words, *"By the word."*

Hebrews 11:3 By faith we understand that the worlds were framed by the word of God, so that the things which are seen were not made of things which are visible.

Psalms 33:6 By the word of the LORD the heavens were made, and all the host of them by the breath of His mouth.

Of Man and Woman

Genesis 1:26,27 Then God said, "Let Us make man in Our image, according to Our likeness; let them have dominion over the fish of the sea, over the birds of the air, and over the cattle, over all the earth and over every creeping thing that creeps on the earth." So God created man in His own image; in the image of God He created him; male and female He created them.

Genesis 2:7 And the LORD God formed man of the dust of the ground, and breathed into his nostrils the breath of life; and man became a living being.

The book of Job is thought to be the oldest book in the Bible. Job had no doubt as to his origin.

Job 10:8a Your hands have made me and fashioned me, an intricate unity ...

Purpose of Creation
➢ *Fulfill Father's Heart*

God planned the creation of mankind to fulfill the Father's heart for an eternal family. He desired a bride for His Son and an everlasting family through which He could duplicate Himself. God created men and women to have an eternal love relationship and intimate fellowship with Himself.

Ephesians 2:4-7 But God, who is rich in mercy, because of His great love with which He loved us, even when we were dead in trespasses, made us alive together with Christ (by grace you have been saved), and raised us up together, and made us sit together in the heavenly places in Christ Jesus, that in the ages to come He might show the exceeding riches of His grace in His kindness toward us in Christ Jesus.

➤ *Fulfill His Eternal Purpose*

He created mankind to fulfill His eternal purpose.

Ephesians 1:9-11 Having made known to us the mystery of His will, according to His good pleasure which He purposed in Himself, that in the dispensation of the fullness of the times He might gather together in one all things in Christ, both which are in heaven and which are on earth–in Him, in whom also we have obtained an inheritance, being predestined according to the purpose of Him who works all things according to the counsel of His will ...

➤ *To Fulfill Himself in Praise and Worship*

He created mankind to be fulfilling to Himself as they ministered to Him in praise and worship.

Isaiah 43:7,21 Everyone who is called by My name, whom I have created for My glory; I have formed him, yes, I have made him.

This people I have formed for Myself; they shall declare My praise.

God had a great eternal purpose when He created mankind in His image. However, God's creative miracles didn't stop with the creation of the heavens and the earth, or with the creation of mankind. They continued all through the Old Testament. God created manna and water in the desert. He created oil and meal for the widow of Zarephath.

MIRACLES OF JUDGMENT

There are many examples of God's judgment in the Bible.
➤ The flood was judgment on the whole earth.
➤ The destruction of Sodom and Gomorrah was judgment on one area.
➤ The judgment on Nadab and Abihu was on men who offered strange, unauthorized fire on the altar. These men took a stand against God's anointed leaders and were destroyed by fire.
➤ Leprosy coming on Gehazi, Elisha's servant was judgment on one man.

Punishment for sin gives people an opportunity to repent.

Why Judgment Comes

There are three reasons why judgment comes.
➤ As punishment for sins

2 Peter 2:9,10a The LORD knows how to deliver the godly out of temptations and to reserve the unjust under punishment for the day of judgment, and especially those who walk according to the flesh in the lust of uncleanness and despise authority.

➤ As an example to later generations

2 Peter 2:6 ... and turning the cities of Sodom and Gomorrah into ashes, condemned them to destruction, making them an example to those who afterward would live ungodly ...

➤ Gives an opportunity to repent

Revelation 9:20,21 But the rest of mankind, who were not killed by these plagues, did not repent of the works of their hands, that they should not worship demons, and idols of gold, silver, brass, stone, and wood, which can neither see nor hear nor walk; and they did not repent of their murders or their sorceries or their sexual immorality or their thefts.

The apostle Peter mentions several miraculous judgments, and used them as proof of God's ability to preserve the godly even in time of judgment.

2 Peter 2:5-9 And did not spare the ancient world, but saved Noah, one of eight people, a preacher of righteousness, bringing in the flood on the world of the ungodly;

And turning the cities of Sodom and Gomorrah into ashes, condemned them to destruction, making them an example to those who afterward would live ungodly; and delivered righteous Lot, who was oppressed with the filthy conduct of the wicked (for that righteous man, dwelling among them, tormented his righteous soul from day to day by seeing and hearing their lawless deeds) ...

Then the LORD knows how to deliver the godly out of temptations and to reserve the unjust under punishment for the day of judgment ...

JUDGMENT – THE FLOOD

Reference: Genesis 6,7

The miracles of God can be wondrous happenings, or they can be terrible ones of judgment. Because of the sinfulness of mankind, God brought the flood to cover the face of the earth. However, in this dreadful judgment, God showed mercy and preserved His created beings – the animals, birds, and men and women.

The flood was God's judgment on the whole earth and mankind.

Genesis 7:19-23 And the waters prevailed exceedingly on the earth, and all the high hills under the whole heaven were covered. The waters prevailed fifteen cubits upward, and the mountains were covered. And all flesh died that moved on the earth: birds and cattle and beasts and every creeping thing that creeps on the earth, and every man. All in whose nostrils was the breath of the spirit of life, all that was on the dry land, died. So He destroyed all living things which were on the face of the ground: both man and cattle, creeping thing and birds of the air. They were destroyed from the earth. Only Noah and those who were with him in the ark remained alive.

Perversion of Human Race

Why did a loving heavenly Father destroy so much of His creation? Was God just *"fed up"* with a sinful people, or was it something He was forced to do?

From the time God promised *"the Seed of the woman"* would crush his head, Satan's plans and purposes were the destruction of all the seed of the woman. We read in Genesis 6 about the perversion that had come on the earth.

Genesis 6:1,2,4 Now it came to pass, when men began to multiply on the face of the earth, and daughters were born to them, that the sons of God saw the daughters of men, that they were beautiful; and they took wives for themselves of all whom they chose.

There were giants on the earth in those days, and also afterward, when the sons of God came in to the daughters of men and they bore children to them. Those were the mighty men who were of old, men of renown.

There is every reason to believe that the *"sons of God"* mentioned are not human sons but angelic creatures. In Job 1-6 and 38:7 *"sons of God,"* refers to angelic and demonic beings only – not humans.

The Genesis account continues,

Genesis 6:5,7 Then the LORD saw that the wickedness of man was great in the earth, and that every intent of the thoughts of his heart was only evil continually.

So the LORD said, "I will destroy man whom I have created from the face of the earth, both man and beast, creeping thing and birds of the air, for I am sorry that I have made them."

Noah and Family Spared

Why were Noah and his family spared? The Bible says,

Genesis 6:8,9 But Noah found grace in the eyes of the LORD. This is the genealogy of Noah. Noah was a just man, perfect in his generations. Noah walked with God.

Notice the words *"perfect in his generations."* There was no corruption in his genealogy with the union of the sons of God and the daughters of men.

The flood didn't come because God was angry at men and women and wanted to destroy them. It came because the human line had become perverted. If Satan's plan hadn't been stopped, there would have been no pure generation through which the *"Seed of the woman"* could come.

Protection in Time of Judgment

➢ *Through Obedience*

God spoke to Noah and Noah obeyed. For 120 years Noah continued to obey God, while the corrupt society around him mocked him. He built the ark by God's exact specifications. Genesis 6:14-16 gives us these instructions.

➢ *Animals Came*

Have you ever wondered what the people who mocked Noah must have thought as two of all the animals of the world began to march through their land toward the ark? God called the animals to the ark, and He preserved them from the evil society they had to pass through. What a miracle that was, and what a sign to the unbelieving world it could have been if they had only believed.

Waters Came

Genesis 7:4 "For after seven more days I will cause it to rain on the earth forty days and forty nights, and I will destroy from the face of the earth all living things that I have made."

Genesis 7:12 And the rain was on the earth forty days and forty nights.

Miraculous Wind

Genesis 8:1 Then God remembered Noah, and every living thing, and all the animals that were with him in the ark. And God made a wind to pass over the earth, and the waters subsided.

Genesis 8:2 The fountains of the deep and the windows of heaven were also stopped, and the rain from heaven was restrained.

God's Promise – The Rainbow

False religions have tried to take the rainbow as their symbol, but God gave the rainbow as a promise to all mankind.

Genesis 8:22 *"While the earth remains, seedtime and harvest, and cold and heat, and winter and summer, and day and night shall not cease."*

Genesis 9:11-13 *"Thus I establish My covenant with you: never again shall all flesh be cut off by the waters of the flood; never again shall there be a flood to destroy the earth."* And God said: *"This is the sign of the covenant which I make between Me and you, and every living creature that is with you, for perpetual generations: I set My rainbow in the cloud, and it shall be for the sign of the covenant between Me and the earth."*

JUDGMENT – DESTRUCTION OF SODOM AND GOMORRAH

Reference: Genesis 18:17-19

There are several things that happened before the destruction of Sodom and Gomorrah which were important parts of this incident. God made a visit to Abraham.

God Talks with Abraham

Genesis 18:17,18 And the LORD said, "Shall I hide from Abraham what I am doing, since Abraham shall surely become a great and mighty nation, and all the nations of the earth shall be blessed in him?"

As God began to reveal to Abraham what was going to happen, He reminded Abraham of his position – all the nations of the earth were to be blessed in him. The Lord continued,

Genesis 18:20,21 And the LORD said, "Because the outcry against Sodom and Gomorrah is great, and because their sin is very grievous, I will go down now and see whether they have done altogether according to the outcry against it that has come to Me; and if not, I will know."

Why did God tell Abraham what He was going to do?

So that Abraham could move into his position of being a blessing to the nations and begin to intercede for the protection of the righteous of the cities. God was covenant-bound to tell Abraham that He was thinking of destroying a nation.

Misunderstood Lot

Many have been quick to condemn Lot. Why was he living in cities that were so evil? Many have thought he was preserved just because he was Abraham's nephew. But the apostle Peter wrote some interesting words about the destruction of Sodom and Gomorrah and about Lot.

2 Peter 2:6-8 And turning the cities of Sodom and Gomorrah into ashes, condemned them to destruction, making them an example to those who afterward would live ungodly; and delivered righteous Lot, who was oppressed with the filthy conduct of the wicked (for that righteous man, dwelling among them, tormented his righteous soul from day to day by seeing and hearing their lawless deeds) ...

Remember when God spoke to Abraham, he spoke of the outcry being very great against these cities because their sin was very grievous. Who was making that outcry?

Ezekiel refers to *those who have charge over the city* in Ezekiel 9:1,2. Daniel refers to the *"watchers"* in Daniel 4:13 and 17. The angels assigned to Sodom and Gomorrah may have been crying out. They may also have been the ones who came into the city to bring Lot and his family out.

However, Peter tells us that Lot was a righteous man tormented day by day seeing and hearing their lawless deeds.

Lot recognized the goodness of the angels when they came into the city and demanded they come into his home for protection.

Genesis 19:2,3a And he said, "Here now, my LORDS, please turn in to your servant's house and spend the night, and wash your feet; then you may rise early and go on your way."

And they said, "No, but we will spend the night in the open square." But he insisted strongly.

Genesis 19:4 Now before they lay down, the men of the city, the men of Sodom, both old and young, all the people from every quarter, surrounded the house.

God has made it clear in this account that all the men of the city, both old and young, from every quarter, surrounded the house. The sin of homosexuality was throughout the city.

Genesis 19:8 "See now, I have two daughters who have not known a man; please, let me bring them out to you, and you may do to them as you wish; only do nothing to these men, since this is the reason they have come under the shadow of my roof."

Lot offered them his two daughters instead. We don't know why it is recorded he did this. Perhaps it was because he knew how evil these men were, and he was proving it by his offer – an offer he knew they would refuse.

Their answer is very interesting.

Genesis 19:9a Then they said, "This one came in to sojourn, and he keeps acting as a judge ..."

They knew where Lot stood. *He keeps acting as a judge ...* God had a witness in Sodom and Gomorrah before He destroyed them. That witness was ignored, oppressed, and tormented.

Protection in Time of Judgment

Genesis 19:15,16 When the morning dawned, the angels urged Lot to hurry, saying, "Arise, take your wife and your two daughters who are here, lest you be consumed in the punishment of the city." And while he lingered, the men took hold of his hand, his wife's hand, and the hands of his two daughters, the LORD being merciful to him, and they brought him out and set him outside the city.

Why were Lot, his wife, and daughters transported, or set outside of the city? Because Lot was a righteous man, and also because Abraham had interceded for them.

Genesis 19:29 And it came to pass, when God destroyed the cities of the plain, that God remembered Abraham, and sent Lot out of the midst of the overthrow, when He overthrew the cities in which Lot had dwelt.

God told Abraham what was going to happen, and Abraham interceded for Lot. Today, it is just as important that we hear from God, and intercede for others.

The Cities Destroyed

Genesis 19:24,26 Then the LORD rained brimstone and fire on Sodom and Gomorrah, from the LORD out of the heavens. So He overthrew those cities, all the plain, all the inhabitants of the cities, and what grew on the ground.

Even in the complete destruction of these cities, God had a purpose other than their destruction. They were to be an example of God's judgment on those who would live ungodly lives.

2 Peter 2:6 And turning the cities of Sodom and Gomorrah into ashes, condemned them to destruction, making them an example to those who afterward would live ungodly.

Jesus Mentioned Incident

When Jesus was asked when the kingdom of God would come, He referred to the time of Sodom and Gomorrah.

Luke 17:28-30 Likewise as it was also in the days of Lot: they ate, they drank, they bought, they sold, they planted, they built; but on the day that Lot went out of Sodom it rained fire and brimstone from heaven and destroyed them all. Even so will it be in the day when the Son of Man is revealed.

COMING JUDGMENT

Before God brings judgment, He always warns the people. For over a hundred years, Noah built the ark. The people laughed at him when he said a great flood was coming and the earth was going to be destroyed. Even when the animals supernaturally gathered, marching across the land, the people didn't believe.

Lot lived in the wicked cities of Sodom and Gomorrah, and they laughed at him. On the last night for those cities, when he went to the homes of his daughters, even his sons-in-law laughed at him and thought he was joking.

Once again, the evilness of the times of Noah, and of the times of Lot, are rampant in our lands. We are the witness to our generations. We too have an obligation to warn them of the coming judgment of God.

Ezekiel 3:18 "When I say to the wicked, `You shall surely die,' and you give him no warning, nor speak to warn the wicked from his wicked way, to save his life, that same wicked man shall die in his iniquity; but his blood I will require at your hand."

Even in the times of judgment, just as God preserved Noah and Lot, He will preserve us. We can say with the prophet Habakkuk,

Habakkuk 3:17-19 Though the fig tree may not blossom, nor fruit be on the vines; though the labor of the olive may fail, and the fields yield no food; though the flock be cut off from the fold, and there be no herd in the stalls—yet I will rejoice in the LORD, will joy in the God of my salvation. The LORD God is my strength; he will make my feet like deer's feet, and He will make me walk on my high hills.

QUESTIONS FOR REVIEW

1. According to this lesson, what is a miracle?

2. What was God's purpose in creating mankind?

3. What reason did the authors give for the destruction of all mankind, except for Noah and his family, in the flood?

Lesson Nine

Miracles of Provision

The miracles of God can affect the whole world, a nation, a situation, a family, or a person. They can be awesome, or almost commonplace. As we have seen, they may bring judgment, but they are also for provision.

There are two things we must do to receive God's miracles of provision. We must hear from God and then we must act in faith on what He has said.

CHILDREN OF ISRAEL IN DESERT

There is no clearer picture of God's miraculous provision for His people than a study of the children of Israel in the wilderness. There were over a million people on this journey. We are told in the book of Numbers there were over 603,550 men, not including the tribe of Levi, or the women and children.

Numbers 1:46,47b All who were numbered were six hundred and three thousand five hundred and fifty. But the Levites were not numbered among them ...

Supernatural Guidance

When the children of Israel began their journey out of Egypt, God went before them in a pillar of fire by night and of cloud by day.

Exodus 13:21,22 And the LORD went before them by day in a pillar of cloud to lead the way, and by night in a pillar of fire to give them light, so as to go by day and night. He did not take away the pillar of cloud by day or the pillar of fire by night from before the people.

Imagine how wonderful it must have been. As they traveled by night, they could see where they were going. When they made camp, they could see to prepare their food. The desert can be very cold at night and they had warmth.

During the day, when the desert sun can be unbearably hot, they were under the coolness of the cloud. David described this time.

Psalms 105:39 He spread a cloud for a covering, and fire to give light in the night.

Since the cloud is described as both a pillar and a covering, it may well have "mushroomed" over them like the tremendous explosions we have seen in pictures.

Supernatural Protection

> ➤ *A Cloud Barrier*

When the Egyptians changed their minds and came after them, it seemed the Israelites were trapped with mountains to the sides of them and the Red Sea in front. Instead of looking at the cloud and knowing they were where God had placed them, that they were in God's protection, they were afraid and began to cry out against Moses.

Exodus 14:13,14 And Moses said to the people, "Do not be afraid. Stand still, and see the salvation of the LORD, which He will accomplish for you today. For the Egyptians whom you see today, you shall see again no more forever. The LORD will fight for you, and you shall hold your peace."

What did God do? He moved the pillar of cloud so that it was between the Egyptians and the Israelites. One side was a light to the children of Israel, the other darkness to the Egyptians. Then God divided the sea and His people crossed to the other side on dry land.

Exodus 14:19-22 And the Angel of God, who went before the camp of Israel, moved and went behind them; and the pillar of cloud went from before them and stood behind them. So it came between the camp of the Egyptians and the camp of Israel. Thus it was a cloud and darkness to the one, and it gave light by night to the other, so that the one did not come near the other all that night.

> ➤ *Parting of Sea*

Then Moses stretched out his hand over the sea; and the LORD caused the sea to go back by a strong east wind all that night, and made the sea into dry land, and the waters were divided. So the children of Israel went into the midst of the sea on the dry ground, and the waters were a wall to them on their right hand and on their left.

God didn't stop with just allowing His people to get away from the Egyptians. He allowed judgment to fall on the Egyptians so they could no longer continue to pursue the children of Israel.

Exodus 14:23,24 And the Egyptians pursued and went after them into the midst of the sea, all Pharaoh's horses, his chariots, and his horsemen.

Now it came to pass, in the morning watch, that the LORD looked down upon the army of the Egyptians through the pillar of fire and cloud, and He troubled the army of the Egyptians.

> ➤ *Delaying Tactics*

When the Egyptians were in the midst of the sea, God caused the wheels to come off their chariots and delayed them.

vs. 25-28 And He took off their chariot wheels, so that they drove them with difficulty; and the Egyptians said, "Let us flee from the face of Israel, for the LORD fights for them against the Egyptians."

Then the LORD said to Moses, "Stretch out your hand over the sea, that the waters may come back upon the Egyptians, on their chariots, and on their horsemen."

And Moses stretched out his hand over the sea; and when the morning appeared, the sea returned to its full depth, while the Egyptians were fleeing into it. So the LORD overthrew the Egyptians in the midst of the sea. Then the waters returned and covered the chariots, the horsemen, and all the army of Pharaoh that came into the sea after them. Not so much as one of them remained.

Often there are two sides to a miracle. To those who belong to the Lord, there is protection. To those who are fighting against the Lord, or against His people, there is judgment.

➤ *Standard of God's Power*

This miracle was the standard of the power of God referred to throughout the Old Testament.

2 Kings 17:36 ... but the LORD, who brought you up from the land of Egypt with great power and an outstretched arm, Him you shall fear, Him you shall worship, and to Him you shall offer sacrifice.

Supernatural Health

Jehovah means the God who reveals Himself. And God revealed Himself as Jehovah-Rapha soon after the Israelites crossed the Red Sea.

Exodus 15:25b,26 There He made a statute and an ordinance for them. And there He tested them, and said, "If you diligently heed the voice of the LORD your God and do what is right in His sight, give ear to His commandments and keep all His statutes, I will put (permit) none of the diseases on you which I have brought (permitted) on the Egyptians. For I am the LORD who heals you."

In Deuteronomy, we find that even in walking over the desert, their feet didn't swell.

Deuteronomy 8:4b ... nor did your foot swell these forty years.

Later, David wrote there wasn't one feeble person among all their tribes.

Psalms 105:37b And there was none feeble among His tribes.

Supernatural Food

➤ *Manna and Quail*

God supernaturally provided food for the journey.

Exodus 16:12b,15 `At twilight you shall eat meat, and in the morning you shall be filled with bread. And you shall know that I am the Lord your God.'

So it was that quails came up at evening and covered the camp, and in the morning the dew lay all around the camp. And when the layer of dew lifted, there, on the surface of the wilderness, was a small round substance, as fine as frost on the ground.

So when the children of Israel saw it, they said to one another, "What is it?" For they did not know what it was. And Moses said to them, "This is the bread which the Lord has given you to eat."

This supernatural provision of food continued for forty years.

Exodus 16:35 And the children of Israel ate manna forty years, until they came to an inhabited land; they ate manna until they came to the border of the land of Canaan.

Supernatural Water

God supernaturally provided water. The first time was at Marah where the water was bitter and God told Moses to cast a certain tree into it.

Exodus 15:25a So he cried out to the Lord, and the Lord showed him a tree; and when he cast it into the waters, the waters were made sweet.

God provided water another time at Rephidim. This time, He instructed Moses to strike the rock.

Exodus 17:6 "Behold, I will stand before you there on the rock in Horeb; and you shall strike the rock, and water will come out of it, that the people may drink." And Moses did so in the sight of the elders of Israel.

For forty years, the children of Israel had water in the wilderness. Sometimes it was a healing of the water, sometimes it was water from a rock, sometimes it was from wells which they dug.

The apostle Paul gives us a summary of this time. He refers to the spiritual drink that followed them.

1 Corinthians 10:1-4 Moreover, brethren, I do not want you to be unaware that all our fathers were under the cloud, all passed through the sea, all were baptized into Moses in the cloud and in the sea, all ate the same spiritual food, and all drank the same spiritual drink. For they drank of that spiritual Rock that followed them, and that Rock was Christ.

Supernatural Clothing

The tribe of Israel wasn't a poor, half-starved group of people struggling through the wilderness in rags. They left Egypt with the wealth of the land.

When God first spoke to Moses, He promised him that his people wouldn't go out empty-handed. The Bible says they "plundered the land." That means as victors, they took the spoils.

Exodus 3:21,22 " And I will give this people favor in the sight of the Egyptians; and it shall be, when you go, that you shall not go empty-handed. But every woman shall ask of her neighbor, namely, of her who dwells near her house, articles of silver, articles of gold, and clothing; and you shall put them on your sons and on your daughters. So you shall plunder the Egyptians."

What did God tell them to do with the clothing? He told them to put it on their sons and daughters. The clothing that supernaturally didn't wear out in the desert was not the rags of slavery, but the garments of the wealthy of Egypt.

Deuteronomy 8:4a Your garments did not wear out on you.

The children of Israel not only left with the plunder of Egypt, they left with flocks and herds.

Exodus 12:31,32 Then he called for Moses and Aaron by night, and said, "Rise and go out from among my people, both you and the children of Israel. And go, serve the LORD as you have said. Also take your flocks and your herds, as you have said, and be gone; and bless me also."

A Conspicuous Sign

As over a million people traveled through the wilderness for forty years, there were conspicuous signs of God's blessing. The pillar of cloud and fire, the manna, and the quail, are a few examples.

For us, the most important thing to realize is that God can and will take care of His people. When times are hard, we should remember that God doesn't change. When there is a need, God still has supernatural provision for His people if they will believe.

MIRACLES THROUGH ELIJAH

The miracles continue all through the Bible. In First Kings, we are given the miracles of Elijah. We will mention only a few of them.

Fed by Ravens

Elijah spoke God's judgment on the nation and proclaimed a drought. Then God led him to hide by the Brook Cherith, where he was supernaturally fed by ravens.

1 Kings 17:1-4,6 And Elijah the Tishbite, of the inhabitants of Gilead, said to Ahab, "As the LORD God of Israel lives, before whom I stand, there shall not be dew nor rain these years, except at my word."

Then the word of the LORD came to him, saying, "Get away from here and turn eastward, and hide by the Brook Cherith, which flows into the Jordan. And it will be that you shall drink from the brook, and I have commanded the ravens to feed you there."

The ravens brought him bread and meat in the morning, and bread and meat in the evening; and he drank from the brook.

Miraculous Flour and Oil

When the brook dried up, God sent him to a widow in Zarephath. He asked her to prepare water and food for him and gave her this promise from the Lord.

1 Kings 17:14 "For thus says the LORD God of Israel: `The bin of flour shall not be used up, nor shall the jar of oil run dry, until the day the LORD sends rain on the earth.' "

The drought continued for three years and six months, and God's supernatural provision continued for Elijah, the widow, and her son. Even to the point of God giving life back to her son when he died during this time.

James 5:17 Elijah was a man with a nature like ours, and he prayed earnestly that it would not rain; and it did not rain on the land for three years and six months.

The apostle James said Elijah had a nature like ours. How encouraging it is to us to know that Elijah was a normal human being operating in the supernatural just as we are to do!

Supernatural Sacrifice

For three years and six months, Elijah had been hiding. Ahab had been searching everywhere to find and kill him. During this time, Ahab had killed many other prophets of the Lord, but God still sent Elijah back to Ahab.

1 Kings 18:17-20 Then it happened, when Ahab saw Elijah, that Ahab said to him, "Is that you, O troubler of Israel?"

And he answered, "I have not troubled Israel, but you and your father's house have, in that you have forsaken the commandments of the LORD, and you have followed the Baals. Now therefore, send and gather all Israel to me on Mount Carmel, the four hundred and fifty prophets of Baal, and the four hundred prophets of Asherah, who eat at Jezebel's table."

So Ahab sent for all the children of Israel, and gathered the prophets together on Mount Carmel.

➢ *850 Versus 1*

Mount Carmel is a small mountain in the plains of northern Israel. As the people stood on its sides, they could easily see everything that happened on the flat mountain top.

The Biblical account is so exciting (See 1 Kings 18)! The false priests prepared their sacrifices in the morning and began to call on their gods to send fire and consume it. By afternoon they were working themselves into a frenzy – cutting themselves and begging their god to answer. As 850 priests were doing this, one man, Elijah stood alone mocking them.

In the evening, Elijah prepared his sacrifice, and had the people pour water over it three times. There was so much water, it ran down from the sacrifice and filled the ditches around the altar. Then Elijah prayed one short prayer.

1 Kings 18:36,37 And it came to pass, at the time of the offering of the evening sacrifice, that Elijah the prophet came near and said, "Lord God of Abraham, Isaac, and Israel, let it be known this day that You are God in Israel, and that I am Your servant, and that I have done all these things at Your word. Hear me, O Lord, hear me, that this people may know that You are the Lord God, and that You have turned their hearts back to You again."

➤ *The Lord is God!*

What happened? The fire of the Lord fell and burned the sacrifice, the wood, the stones of the altar, and the water. The people of Israel saw it and fell down and worshiped God.

1 Kings 18:38,39 Then the fire of the Lord fell and consumed the burnt sacrifice, and the wood and the stones and the dust, and it licked up the water that was in the trench. Now when all the people saw it, they fell on their faces; and they said, "The Lord, He is God! The Lord, He is God!"

What an awesome series of miracles. First God spoke through Elijah pronouncing the drought. Then He protected him through the drought for over three years. Then He proved Himself miraculously by sending the fire.

First Kings is full of the miracles performed through Elijah.

MIRACLES THROUGH ELISHA

Elisha was a disciple of Elijah and when Elijah was leaving this earth, Elisha asked for a double portion of power. The miracles continued unabated through him, and there are twice as many miracles recorded just as he asked.

Elijah parted the Jordan River, Elisha parted the Jordan River. Elijah had an increase of flour and oil, Elisha had a miraculous increase of oil.

Increase of Widow's Oil

2 Kings 4:1-7 A certain woman of the wives of the sons of the prophets cried out to Elisha, saying, "Your servant my husband is dead, and you know that your servant feared the LORD. And the creditor is coming to take my two sons to be his slaves."

So Elisha said to her, "What shall I do for you? Tell me, what do you have in the house?"

And she said, "Your maidservant has nothing in the house but a jar of oil."

Then he said, "Go, borrow vessels from everywhere, from all your neighbors–empty vessels; do not gather just a few. And when you have come in, you shall shut the door behind you and your sons; then pour it into all those vessels, and set aside the full ones."

So she went from him and shut the door behind her and her sons, who brought the vessels to her; and she poured it out. Now it came to pass, when the vessels were full, that she said to her son, "Bring me another vessel." And he said to her, "There is not another vessel." So the oil ceased.

Then she came and told the man of God.

And he said, "Go, sell the oil and pay your debt; and you and your sons live on the rest."

In this miracle of provision, the woman received exactly what she had faith to receive. She was told to borrow vessels – not a few, and that they would be filled with oil. The amount she borrowed in faith, was the amount of oil she received.

The book of Second Kings is full of the miracles that happened during the time of Elisha.

MIRACLES OF SUPERNATURAL HEALING

Throughout the Old Testament, there is a continuous record of miracles of healing.

Miriam's Leprosy

Miriam was the sister of Moses and Aaron. She was part of the leadership of the children of Israel. She led them in praise for what God had done in leading them through the Red Sea and destroying their enemies. But Miriam, along with Aaron, let a critical spirit come in and spoke against Moses in two ways. One was concerning his marriage to an Ethiopian woman. The other was concerning his leadership of the children of Israel.

The Bible makes it clear that leprosy came on her as a result of her sin.

Numbers 12:1,2 Then Miriam and Aaron spoke against Moses because of the Ethiopian woman whom he had married; for he had married an Ethiopian woman. And they said, "Has the LORD indeed spoken only through Moses? Has He not spoken through us also?" And the LORD heard it.

vs. 9,10 So the anger of the LORD was aroused against them, and He departed. And when the cloud departed from above the tabernacle, suddenly Miriam became leprous, as white as snow. Then Aaron turned toward Miriam, and there she was, a leper.

What did Miriam and Aaron do when they saw the leprosy? Aaron immediately confessed their sin and asked for her healing.

Numbers 12:11-14 So Aaron said to Moses, "Oh, my LORD! Please do not lay this sin on us, in which we have done foolishly and in which we have sinned. Please do not let her be as one dead, whose flesh is half consumed when he comes out of his mother's womb!"

So Moses cried out to the LORD, saying, "Please heal her, O God, I pray!" Then the LORD said to Moses, "If her father had but spit in her face, would she not be shamed seven days? Let her be shut out of the camp seven days, and after that she may be received again."

Naaman's Leprosy

Naaman being healed of leprosy is one of the most interesting miracles in the Old Testament. Why did Elisha refuse to see him, and tell him through a servant to dip in the river Jordan seven times?

We know that Naaman was great, honorable, and a mighty man of valor. He was the commander of the army of Syria, and because of him, the Lord had given victory to the Syrian army.

2 Kings 5:1 Now Naaman, commander of the army of the king of Syria, was a great and honorable man in the eyes of his master, because by him the LORD had given victory to Syria. He was also a mighty man of valor, but he was a leper.

Naaman's wife had a slave girl from Israel, and she knew about the prophet of Israel and his great power.

2 Kings 5:3 Then she said to her mistress, "If only my master were with the prophet who is in Samaria! For he would heal him of his leprosy."

Naaman went to his king and asked permission to go to the prophet of Israel. But when he brought a letter from the king of Syria to the king of Israel, he thought they were trying to make an excuse for war. However, Elisha heard about Naaman and sent for him.

2 Kings 5:8-12 So it was, when Elisha the man of God heard that the king of Israel had torn his clothes, that he sent to the king, saying, "Why have you torn your clothes? Please let him come to me, and he shall know that there is a prophet in Israel."

Then Naaman went with his horses and chariot, and he stood at the door of the house of Elisha. And Elisha sent a messenger to him, saying, "Go and wash in the Jordan seven times, and your flesh shall be restored to you, and you shall be clean."

But Naaman became furious, and went away and said, "Indeed, I said to myself, `He will surely come out to me, and stand and call on the name of the LORD his God, and wave his hand over the place, and heal the leprosy.' Are not the Abanah and the Pharpar, the rivers of Damascus, better than all the waters of Israel? Could I not wash in them and be clean?" So he turned and went away in a rage.

Naaman had pictured to himself how he would be healed. It was a picture befitting his position. He had his own pattern, but God spoke to Elisha and told him what to do and to say.

v. 13,14 And his servants came near and spoke to him, and said, "My father, if the prophet had told you to do something great, would you not have done it? How much more then, when he says to you, `Wash, and be clean'?"

So he went down and dipped seven times in the Jordan, according to the saying of the man of God; and his flesh was restored like the flesh of a little child, and he was clean.

Even though Naaman believed enough to come to the prophet, he must have come with his entourage in pride. We know he came with wealth expecting to pay the prophet.

2 Kings 5:5b So he departed and took with him ten talents of silver, six thousand shekels of gold, and ten changes of clothing.

To be healed it was necessary for him to be obedient and to humble himself. The results were his complete healing in the physical, but more important, his acceptance of the Lord as his God.

2 Kings 5:17 So Naaman said, "Then, if not, please let your servant be given two mule-loads of earth; for your servant will no longer offer either burnt offering or sacrifice to other gods, but to the LORD."

King Hezekiah

The nation of Israel had become divided when Hezekiah became king over Judah. The Bible gives us a very descriptive summary of his reign.

2 Kings 18:5-7a He trusted in the LORD God of Israel, so that after him was none like him among all the kings of Judah, nor any who were before him. For he held fast to the LORD; he did not depart from following Him, but kept His commandments, which the LORD had commanded Moses. The LORD was with him; he prospered wherever he went.

After fourteen years of being king, he was sick to the point of death.

2 Kings 20:1 In those days Hezekiah was sick and near death. And Isaiah the prophet, the son of Amoz, went to him and said to him, "Thus says the LORD: `Set your house in order, for you shall die, and not live.'"

When Hezekiah heard that he was going to die, he reminded the Lord of how he had been a good king and walked before the Lord in truth and loyalty.

2 Kings 20:2,3 Then he turned his face toward the wall, and prayed to the LORD, saying, "Remember now, O LORD, I pray, how I have walked before You in truth and with a loyal heart, and have done what was good in Your sight." And Hezekiah wept bitterly.

vs. 4-6 Then it happened, before Isaiah had gone out into the middle court, that the word of the LORD came to him, saying, "Return and tell Hezekiah the leader of My people, `Thus says the LORD, the God of David your father: I have heard your prayer, I have seen your tears; surely I will heal you. On the third day you shall go upto the house of the LORD. And I will add to your days fifteen years. I will deliver you and this city from the hand of the king of Assyria; and I will defend this city for My own sake, and for the sake of My servant David.'"

Hezekiah wasn't satisfied with the word of the Lord through Isaiah, he wanted a sign. Then he wanted a more difficult sign. God did everything Hezekiah asked of Him – even to making the shadow of the sun go backwards on the sun dial.

2 Kings 20:8 -11 And Hezekiah said to Isaiah, "What is the sign that the LORD will heal me, and that I shall go up to the house of the LORD the third day?"

Then Isaiah said, "This is the sign to you from the LORD, that the LORD will do the thing which He has spoken: shall the shadow go forward ten degrees or go backward ten degrees?"

And Hezekiah answered, "It is an easy thing for the shadow to go down ten degrees; no, but let the shadow go backward ten degrees."

So Isaiah the prophet cried out to the LORD, and He brought the shadow ten degrees backward, by which it had gone down on the sundial of Ahaz.

Summary

So many miracles are told about in the Old Testament. People were resurrected from the dead. People were supernaturally protected from death such as Daniel in the lion's den, and the three men that were thrown into the fiery furnace. There are miracles of protection such as God blinding the eyes of their enemies. There are miracles of provision. One time, God even spoke through a donkey.

The Old Testament is a book of miracles. The God of the Old Testament was a miracle-working God. Those who believed, walked in supernatural power.

The writer of the book of Hebrews states that God is the same yesterday, today, and forever.

Hebrews 13:8 Jesus Christ is the same yesterday, today, and forever.

He is still a miracle working God. If we believe, we can still walk in His supernatural power to face the challenges of our time.

Note: For more study on the miracles of the Old Testament, we recommend All the Miracles of the Bible by Herbert Lockyer, Zondervan Publishing Company. (We also recommend you ignore the few paragraphs where he tries to explain why miracles have ceased – they haven't!)

QUESTIONS FOR REVIEW

1. List some of the miracles of provision that were conspicuous signs of God's supernatural blessing upon the children of Israel as they traveled through the wilderness.

2. List some of the supernatural miracles that happened in the life and ministry of Elijah.

3. List some of the supernatural miracles that happened in the life and ministry of Elisha.

Possessing Our Inheritance

CROSSING INTO CANAAN

Day after day, the people of Israel had seen and experienced the power of God on their behalf. Finally, they came to the border of Canaan and set up camp.

At the Border

God had given them Cannan, but they had to go in and possess it.

Numbers 13:1-3 And the LORD spoke to Moses, saying, "Send men to spy out the land of Canaan, which I am giving to the children of Israel; from each tribe of their fathers you shall send a man, every one a leader among them."

So Moses sent them from the Wilderness of Paran according to the command of the LORD, all of them men who were heads of the children of Israel.

The Report

As God commanded, Moses sent a leader from each tribe to spy out the land. They spent forty days going through the land, and then they brought back their reports to Moses and the people of Israel.

Numbers 13:27-29 Then they told him, and said: "We went to the land where you sent us. It truly flows with milk and honey, and this is its fruit. Nevertheless the people who dwell in the land are strong; the cities are fortified and very large; moreover we saw the descendants of Anak there. The Amalekites dwell in the land of the South; the Hittites, the Jebusites, and the Amorites dwell in the mountains; and the Canaanites dwell by the sea and along the banks of the Jordan."

Caleb remembered all the Lord had done.

Numbers 13:30 Then Caleb quieted the people before Moses, and said, "Let us go up at once and take possession, for we are well able to overcome it."

Ten of the spies replied,

Numbers 13:31b-33 "We are not able to go up against the people, for they are stronger than we."

And they gave the children of Israel a bad report of the land which they had spied out, saying, "The land through which we have gone as spies is a land that devours its inhabitants, and all the people whom we saw in it are men of great stature. There we saw the giants (the descendants of Anak came from the giants); and we were like grasshoppersin our own sight, and so we were in their sight."

Then Joshua and Caleb tried to encourage the people to believe in the Lord.

Numbers 14:6-11 And Joshua the son of Nun and Caleb the son of Jephunneh, who were among those who had spied out the land, tore their clothes; And they spoke to all the congregation of the children of Israel, saying: "The land we passed through to spy out is an exceedingly good land. If the LORD delights in us, then He will bring us intothis land and give it to us, `a land which flows with milk and honey.' Only do not rebel against the LORD, nor fear the people of the land, for they are our bread; their protection has departed from them, and the LORD is with us. Do not fear them."

The Choice

The people had to make a choice. Who would they believe? Where was their faith?

They chose not to believe in the power of God. Instead, they wanted to stone the people who did. They wanted to stone Moses, Caleb, and Joshua. They wanted to return to the slavery of Egypt.

Numbers 14:10,11 And all the congregation said to stone them with stones. Now the glory of the LORD appeared in the tabernacle of meeting before all the children of Israel. And the LORD said to Moses: "How long will these people reject Me? And how long will they not believe Me, with all the signs which I have performed amongthem?"

For forty years, God let them wander in the wilderness until all the people who had refused to believe in Him and His power had died. Joshua and Caleb didn't die. Again they came to the border of Canaan. Now Joshua was in command.

Still today, many times believers are unwilling to do what the Lord leads them to do. They lack faith or understanding of His will, and He lets them wander in their own wilderness learning more of Him. Then, He brings them back again to the same place of decision.

We must learn to operate in faith and take through faith what the Lord has given us. Unbelief always brings defeat.

Second Time

Again the people of Israel were at the border of Canaan and God said to Joshua,

Joshua 1:6-9 "Be strong and of good courage, for to this people you shall divide as an inheritance the land which I swore to their fathers to give them.

Only be strong and very courageous, that you may observe to do according to all the law which Moses My servant commanded you; do not turn from it to the right hand or to the left, that you may prosper wherever you go.

This Book of the Law shall not depart from your mouth, but you shall meditate in it day and night, that you may observe to do according to all that is written in it. For then you will make your way prosperous, and then you will have good success.

To Guarantee Success:

Meditate on the Law day and night

Be strong

Do not be afraid, or dismayed

For then you will have good success.

Have I not commanded you? Be strong and of good courage; do not be afraid, nor be dismayed, for the LORD your God is with you wherever you go."

Joshua sent out two spies, and their presence was discovered by the king of Jericho. But Rahab, a harlot, who lived on the wall of the city, hid them and let them down by a cord through the window. But notice some of the words Rahab spoke to them.

Joshua 2:9-11 And said to the men: "I know that the LORD has given you the land, that the terror of you has fallen on us, and that all the inhabitants of the land are fainthearted because of you.

For we have heard how the LORD dried up the water of the Red Sea for you when you came out of Egypt, and what you did to the two kings of the Amorites who were on the other side of the Jordan, Sihon and Og, whom you utterly destroyed.

And as soon as we heard these things, our hearts melted; neither did there remain any more courage in anyone because of you, for the LORD your God, He is God in heaven above and on earth beneath."

The enemy knew their strength. It was not in the number of their fighting men, it was in their Lord . The enemy knew what God had done on their behalf before.

These two spies brought back their report,

Joshua 2:24 And they said to Joshua, "Truly the LORD has delivered all the land into our hands, for indeed all the inhabitants of the country are faint-hearted because of us."

Crossing the Jordan River

It was the time of harvest and the Jordan River was overflowing its banks, but to God's people, this was not an obstacle. Joshua told them to sanctify – consecrate, make themselves holy – and that the next day they would see the Lord do wonders.

Joshua 3:5 And Joshua said to the people, "Sanctify yourselves, for tomorrow the LORD will do wonders among you."

What happened? The priests took the ark and as soon as their feet touched the waters of the river, the waters piled up on themselves and the people walked across on dry ground.

Joshua 3:15,16a,17 And as those who bore the ark came to the Jordan, and the feet of the priests who bore the ark dipped in the edge of the water (for the Jordan overflows all its banks during the whole time of harvest), that the waters which came down from upstream stood still, and rose in a heap.

Then the priests who bore the ark of the covenant of the LORD stood firm on dry ground in the midst of the Jordan; and all Israel crossed over on dry ground, until all the people had crossed completely over the Jordan.

Prerequisites of Possessing Inheritance

What was the groundwork for this tremendous miracle?

➤ First, they were to know and meditate on God's Word.

> **This Book of the Law shall not depart from your mouth, but you shall meditate in it day and night, that you may observe to do according to all that is written in it. For then you will make your way prosperous, and then you will have good success (Joshua 1:8).**

➤ Second they were to have faith.

> **Be strong and of good courage; do not be afraid, nor be dismayed, for the LORD your God is with you wherever you go (Joshua 1:9).**

➤ Third, they were to consecrate themselves, to get the sin out of their lives.

➤ Fourth, they had to act on what they believed.

These are still the prerequisites to possessing our inheritance today.

Faith is an action

We must be willing "to get our feet wet," in order to see God accomplish miracles for us.

THE WALLS OF JERICHO

Though the children of Israel were to fight and take the land physically, God had a plan for the battle. The people were to march in silence around the city of Jericho each day for six days following the priests carrying the ark. Seven priests were to blow seven rams horns in front of the ark. The men of war were to march in front of the priests.

On the seventh day, they were to march around the city seven times. Then there would be a loud blast on the horns, and the people were to shout and the walls would fall down flat.

The people did exactly as God had said.

Joshua 6:20b And it happened ... that the wall fell down flat.

Principles of Battle

There are several principles for successful battle in the Spirit from this incident.

➤ We should send spiritually mature men or women of God to find the enemy's weaknesses.

➤ We should pray and listen for God's plan. (This is the only time in history walls have fallen down when people shouted.)

➤ As the priests marched around the city each day carrying the ark, they took God's presence into the situation.

➤ The blowing of the ram's horns by the priests was testifying of how powerful God is and prophesying the victory by the priests.

➤ The shout the people gave on the seventh day, the seventh time around, was a shout of victory – a shout of faith.

SIN BRINGS DEFEAT

First Battle at Ai

The next city to be conquered was Ai and again Joshua sent out two spies. They came back with their report.

Joshua 7:3 And they returned to Joshua and said to him, "Do not let all the people go up, but let about two or three thousand men go up and attack Ai. Do not weary all the people there, for the people of Ai are few."

Joshua and the people listened and sent 3,000 men into the battle.

Joshua 7:4,5 So about three thousand men went up there from the people, but they fled before the men of Ai. And the men of Ai struck down about thirty-six men, for they chased them from before the gate as far as Shebarim, and struck them down on the descent; therefore the hearts of the people melted and became like water.

Joshua and the elders of Israel tore their clothes and threw themselves down on the ground before the ark. "Oh God, how could you let this happen to us? (Does that sound familiar?) We should have stayed on the other side of Jordan. All the people of the land will hear how we have been defeated, and they will destroy us!"

What was God's answer?

Joshua 7:10,11 So the LORD said to Joshua: "Get up! Why do you lie thus on your face? Israel has sinned, and they have also transgressed My covenant which I commanded them. For they have even taken some of the accursed things, and have both stolen and deceived; and they have also put it among their own stuff.

Achan had stolen from the Lord see Joshua 6:19) and the whole nation of Israel fell under the curse. This is an example of corporate responsibility.

v. 12 Therefore the children of Israel could not stand before their enemies, but turned their backs before their enemies, because they have become doomed to destruction. Neither will I be with you anymore, unless you destroy the accursed from among you."

We could paraphrase God's words, "Stand up, Joshua. Where's your faith? I didn't do this to you. There's sin, and because of that sin, the children of Israel couldn't stand before their enemies!"

➤ *Negative Principles*

The people were so certain this was "but a few," they hadn't spent time seeking the Lord's plan. If they had sought Him ahead of time, He would have pointed out the sin and saved them from this defeat. They had said in effect, "Never mind God, we can handle this."

They had not made a complete commitment of everything they had. They sent only a few of the men, only a part had gone to battle.

Sin will always bring defeat, and the only answer to sin is to get totally rid of it.

Second Battle at Ai

After the sin in the camp was gotten rid of, God came to Joshua.

Joshua 8:1-5 Then the LORD said to Joshua: "Do not be afraid, nor be dismayed; take all the people of war with you, and arise, go up to Ai. See, I have given into your hand the king of Ai, his people, his city, and his land ... Lay an ambush for the city behind it."

So Joshua arose, and all the people of war, to go up against Ai; and Joshua chose thirty thousand mighty men of valor and sent them away by night. And he commanded them, saying: "Behold, you shall lie in ambush against the city, behind the city. Do not go very far from the city, but all of you be ready.

"Then I and all the people who are with me will approach the city; and it will come about, when they come out against us as at the first, that we shall flee before them."

Notice how Joshua took their defeat and turned it into victory. *"They will come out after us and they will expect us to flee just as we did before."*

Joshua 8:6,7 "For they will come out after us till we have drawn them from the city, for they will say, `They are fleeing before us as at the first.' Therefore we will flee before them. Then you shall rise from the ambush and seize the city, for the LORD your God will deliver it into your hand."

GIDEON – PLUS GOD

Joshua had died, and the sixth chapter of Judges starts with very discouraging verses. God's chosen race, those who were to represent Him to the rest of the world, were existing in caves and going without food.

Judges 6:1,2,6 And the children of Israel did evil in the sight of the LORD. So the LORD delivered them into the hand of Midian for seven years, and the hand of Midian prevailed against Israel. Because of the Midianites, the children of Israel made for themselves the dens, the caves, and the strongholds which are in the mountains.

So Israel was greatly impoverished because of the Midianites, and the children of Israel cried out to the LORD.

The Bible leaves us no doubt as to why they were in this condition – *They did evil in the sight of the Lord.*

They also did something that was right – they *cried out to the Lord*.

Call of Gideon

What an encouragement Gideon can be to us! He was the youngest in his family. His father worshiped Baal. He was from a nation that was in defeat. And yet, God called him to set his people free.

Gideon was threshing wheat behind the winepress, trying to hide it from the Midianites, when the angel of the Lord came to him.

Judges 6:12 And the Angel of the LORD appeared to him, and said to him, "The LORD is with you, you mighty man of valor!"

Destroying Altars and Symbols

Then Gideon, following the Lord's instructions, with the help of ten young men, cut down the grove beside the altar of Baal, threw down the altar of Baal, built an altar to the Lord and offered a young bullock on that altar using the wood from the grove to burn the sacrifice.

Gideon and his men destroyed the symbol of his people's sin and made an offering to gain access to the Lord .

What does the Bible say happened then?

Judges 6:34,35 But the Spirit of the LORD came upon Gideon; then he blew the trumpet, and the Abiezrites gathered behind him. And he sent messengers throughout all Manasseh, who also gathered behind him. He also sent messengers to Asher, Zebulun, and Naphtali; and they came up to meet them.

Gideon's Army

Too many came to join Gideon, and God said,

Judges 7:2-4a,5-7 And the LORD said to Gideon, "The people who are with you are too many for Me to give the Midianites into their hands, lest Israel claim glory for itself against Me, saying, `My own hand has saved me.'

Now therefore, proclaim in the hearing of the people, saying, `Whoever is fearful and afraid, let him turn and depart at once from Mount Gilead.' And twenty-two thousand of the people returned, and ten thousand remained.

And the LORD said to Gideon, "The people are still too many; bring them down to the water, and I will test them for you there ..."

So he brought the people down to the water. And the LORD said to Gideon, "Everyone who laps from the water with his tongue, as a dog laps, you shall set apart by himself; likewise everyone who gets down on his knees to drink." And the number of those who lapped, putting their hand to their mouth, was three hundred men; but all the rest ofthe people got down on their knees to drink water.

Then the LORD said to Gideon, "By the three hundred men who lapped I will save you, and deliver the Midianites into your hand. Let all the other people go, every man to his place."

Positive Principles

Received their strategy from God

Used enemy's previous experience against them

First God removed from the fighting men those who were afraid. Then He removed any who were not fully alert, ready for battle.

God Understood

God understood Gideon's humanity. He told him to go down against the camp immediately, but if he was afraid to do that, to take another and spy out the camp.

Gideon had three hundred men and the camp below had men like the *"sand of the sea."* Gideon didn't try to bluff a bravery he didn't have. He chose to spy out the camp.

Judges 7:13,14 And when Gideon had come, there was a man telling a dream to his companion. He said, "I have just had a dream: to my surprise, a loaf of barley bread tumbled into the camp of Midian; it came to a tent and struck it so that it fell and overturned, and the tent collapsed."

Then his companion answered and said, "This is nothing else but the sword of Gideon the son of Joash, a man of Israel; for into his hand God has delivered Midian and the whole camp."

A Trumpet, A Torch, A Pitcher

Gideon was encouraged just as God had said. He came back to his men full of faith and said,

Judges 7:15b "Arise, for the LORD has delivered the camp of Midian into your hand."

Judges 7:16-18,20,21 Then he divided the three hundred men into three companies, and he put a trumpet into every man's hand, with empty pitchers, and torches inside the pitchers.

And he said to them, "Look at me and do likewise; watch, and when I come to the edge of the camp you shall do just as I do: when I blow the trumpet, I and all who are with me, then you also blow the trumpets on every side of the whole camp, and say, `The sword of the LORD and of Gideon!'"

Then the three companies blew the trumpets and broke the pitchers–they held the torches in their left hands and the trumpets in their right hands for blowing–and they cried, "The sword of the LORD and of Gideon!"

And every man stood in his place all around the camp; and the whole army ran and cried out and fled.

In the left hand, they held the torches. In the right hand, they held the trumpets. They were not holding human weapons of battle. They won the battle through their supernatural weapons by faith and obedience.

DAVID AND GOLIATH

David, a young man, stood up to the giant Goliath. How did he fight that battle? Read his words.

1 Samuel 17:37a,40,43,45 Moreover David said, "The LORD, who delivered me from the paw of the lion and from the paw of the bear, He will deliver me from the hand of this Philistine."

Then he took his staff in his hand; and he chose for himself five smooth stones from the brook, and put them in a shepherd's bag, in a pouch which he had, and his sling was in his hand. And he drew near to the Philistine.

So the Philistine said to David, "Am I a dog, that you come to me with sticks?" And the Philistine cursed David by his gods.

Then David said to the Philistine, "You come to me with a sword, with a spear, and with a javelin. But I come to you in the name of the LORD of hosts, the God of the armies of Israel, whom you have defied. This day the LORD will deliver you into my hand, and I will strike you and take your head from you. And this day I will givethe carcasses of the camp of the Philistines to the birds of the air and the wild beasts of the earth, that all the earth may know that there is a God in Israel. Then all this assembly shall know that the LORD does not save with sword and spear; for the battle is the LORD'S, and He will give you into our hands."

vs. 48-51 And it was so, when the Philistine arose and came and drew near to meet David, that David hastened and ran toward the army to meet the Philistine.

Then David put his hand in his bag and took out a stone; and he slung it and struck the Philistine in his forehead, so that the stone sank into his forehead, and he fell on his face to the earth. David prevailed over the Philistine with a sling and a stone, and struck the Philistine and killed him. But there was no sword in the hand of David.

Therefore David ran and stood over the Philistine, took his sword and drew it out of its sheath and killed him, and cut off his head with it. And when the Philistines saw that their champion was dead, they fled.

David knew the power of God, and he walked in that power. He spoke in faith praising God for what He had done, and for what He was going to do. He didn't look at outward circumstances.

Summary

There are many things we can learn about present-day warfare from the battles we have studied in the Old Testament.

> God called particular people to fight particular battles. Sometimes we are defeated because it was never God's plan for us to be in a particular battle.

> When we are attacked, or a situation comes to our attention, the first things we should do is go to God in prayer. We must get an understanding of His plan for our situation.

> Is there sin in our life that should be gotten rid of? There can be no compromise with Satan or with his followers. God will speak to us about things that are not right if we allow Him to do so.

> We should spend time praising Him for all the things He has done for us in the past. Not so that we can get God's attention or approval, but so that our own spirit can be built up in remembering the wonderful things He has done.

> Then we should move with faith in God's Word and in His power, to defeat the enemy!

QUESTIONS FOR REVIEW

1. Having seen the same things in the land, why were Caleb and Joshua's reports different from the other ten spies?

2. According to Joshua 2:9-11, why were the people of Jericho afraid of the children of Israel?

3. Give an example from the Old Testament of how the children of Israel possessed their inheritance or won a great spiritual battle by a supernatural manifestation of God's wisdom and power.

Other Courses in This Series

By A.L. and Joyce Gill

The Authority of the Believer – How to Quit Losing and Start Winning

This life-changing study reveals God's provision for mankind's victory and dominion over Satan in the world today. God's eternal purpose for every believer was revealed at creation when God said, *"Let them have dominion!"* You will be released into a powerful new spirit of boldness as you discover how you can start winning in every struggle of life.

God's Provision for Healing – Receiving and Ministering God's Healing Power

This powerful teaching lays a solid Word foundation which releases the faith of the students to receive their own healing, walk in perfect health, and boldly minister healing to others. Many are healed as this revelation comes alive in their spirits.

Supernatural Living – Through the Gifts of the Holy Spirit

Every believer can be released into operating in all nine gifts of the Holy Spirit in their daily lives. From an intimate relationship with the Holy Spirit, each person will discover the joy of walking in the supernatural as the vocal, revelation, and power gifts are released

Praise and Worship – Becoming Worshipers of God

Discover the joy of moving into God's presence and releasing your spirit in all of the powerful, fresh, biblical expressions of high praise and intimate worship to God. As you study God's plan for praise and worship, you will become a daily worshiper of God.

The Church Triumphant – Through the Book of Acts

Jesus announced, *"I will build my Church and the gates of hell will not prevail against it."* This thrilling, topical study of the book of Acts reveals that church in action as a pattern for our lives today. It will inspire us into a new and greater dimension of supernatural living as signs, wonders, and miracles are released.

The Ministry Gifts – Apostles, Prophets, Evangelists, Pastors, Teachers

Jesus gave gifts to men! These precious and important gifts are men and women God has called as His apostles, prophets, evangelists, pastors, and teachers. Discover how these gifts are being restored to His church, and how they function to believers to do the works of Jesus.

New Creation Image – Knowing Who You Are in Christ

This life-changing revelation will free believers from feelings of guilt, condemnation, unworthiness, inferiority and inadequacy, to be conformed to the image of Christ. It will release each believer to enjoy being, doing, and having all for which they were created in God's image.

Miracle Evangelism – God's Plan to Reach the World – By John Ezekiel

A powerful study which will release believers into becoming daily soul winners in the great end-time harvest through miracle evangelism. Like the believers in the book of Acts, we can experience the joy of reaching the lost as God confirms His Word through signs, wonders, and healing miracles.

Many of the manuals are available in other languages: Korean, Russian, and Spanish. There are also teaching tapes and videos that go with most of them.

Call Powerhouse Publishing for more information. 1-800-366-3119